D1710335

CLASSIC STOCK CARS

Dr. John Craft

MBI Publishing Company

First published in 1997 by MBI Publishing Company,
729 Prospect Avenue, PO Box 1, Osceola, WI 54020-0001
USA

MBI Publishing Company books are also available at discounts in bulk quantity for industrial or sales-promotional use. For details write to Special Sales Manager at Motorbooks International, Wholesalers & Distributors, 729 Prospect Avenue, PO Box 1, Osceola, WI 54020-0001 USA

Library of Congress Cataloging-in-Publication Data

Craft, John Albert.
     Classic stock cars / John Craft.
        p. cm.
     Includes Index.
     ISBN 0-7603-0298-7 (pbk. : paper)
     1. Automobiles, Racing. 2. Stock car
     racing--United States--History. 3.
     NASCAR (Association)--History. I. Title.
     TL236.C6924   1997
     769.72'0973--dc21   97-18635

On the front cover: Richard Petty's first car after his 1978 switch from Dodge to Chevrolet was a Monte Carlo.

On the frontispiece: Smokey's Boss was powered by a race-spec 600-horsepower 302-cubic-inch engine. The little powerhouse was topped with two 1,050-cfm Holley Dominator carburetors when it first showed up at his Daytona Beach garage.

On the title page: In July 1969, the factory-backed Aero Wars were in full swing. When the NASCAR tour rolled into Daytona for the Firecracker 400, Ford Talladegas and Mercury Spoiler IIs were the class of the field. Cale Yarborough and Donnie Allison drove that point home by qualifying first and second for the race.

On the back cover: Top: Curtis Turner's 1956 Ford, the "Purple Hog" was powered by a 230-horsepower 312-cubic-inch Y-block engine. **Bottom:** Ernie Irvan's Kodak Film Chevrolet Lumina.

Edited by Mike Dapper
Designed by Katie Finney

Printed in Hong Kong through World Print, Ltd.

Contents

INTRODUCTION

Winston Cup stock car racing is, without a doubt, the most popular form of motorsports competition in the United States today. Modern-day NASCAR (National Association for Stock Car Automobile Racing) events sell out years in advance, and network coverage of every race on the tour draws high ratings every weekend.

But things weren't always that way. Once upon a time not so long ago, stock car racing was primarily a southern phenomenon, which garnered only grudging media coverage outside the region. Nonetheless, NASCAR's earliest seasons were characterized by cars and drivers that possessed both a character and flare that many feel is absent in modern stock car circles. Race cars of the 1950s, 1960s, and 1970s, for example, were far different than their modern counterparts in both configuration and point of origin.

The Big Three were primarily responsible for a race car's configuration in the days when Ike and JFK were in the White House, and wind tunnels, restrictor plates, and Fortune 500 sponsorships were still years in the future. Yet the close-quarters action that thrills modern fans was even then part of the NASCAR program.

Drivers like Fireball Roberts, Richard Petty, and Cale Yarborough duked it out weekly in factory-backed big-block-powered race cars that owed more to the regular-production assembly line than the race fabricator's art. During NASCAR's earliest days, their on-track exploits set a standard that modern-day racers like Ernie Irvan, Dale Earnhardt, and Darrell Waltrip follow until this day. The cars they drove also set a standard of sorts and served as the evolutionary springboard to the super-sleek Thunderbirds, Monte Carlos, and Grand Prixes that make up a modern stock car starting grid.

Unfortunately, time has taken its toll on both the drivers and race cars that helped lay the groundwork for NASCAR's current greatness.

This book was written in the hopes that, though gone, the great drivers and equally great competition cars of NASCAR's past will not be forgotten. What follows is a brief look at more than two dozen of the cars driven into combat during the first four decades of Grand National stock car racing. Along with the text and photos that portray each race car in this volume, the reader will find, as a point of reference, a list of each car's technical specifications. Among them is the qualifying speed for the Southern 500 at Darlington (the only track that hosted all of the cars covered) during the years each was in competition.

PART ONE) THE EARLY YEARS

CURTIS TURNER'S 1956 FORD

Curtis Morton Turner was a NASCAR original. He was born in the timber country of Virginia, and he sought his early fortune in those same Old Dominion state forests. Some of those endeavors involved the woodlands he had been born to, and for a time Turner was a lumber man. Other endeavors simply took place in those woodlands on clear moonlit nights, when he ran carloads of moonshine to the nearest city full of thirsty customers.

Along the way, Turner learned how to handle a high-performance car at speed and to play for high stakes in the business world. Both of those skills served him well later in life. Turner's skill at the helm of a fast car eventually led him to try his hand at the fledgling sport of stock car racing soon after Big Bill France organized the series in 1949. Turner's first NASCAR win came at the fabled Langhorne Speedway in Langhorne, Pennsylvania, during the first season of "strictly stock" competition. By the mid–1950s, his exploits—both on and off the track—made him one of the series' first stars.

Turner was a ruthless competitor once the green flag fell, and his penchant for knocking cars out of his racing path soon earned him the nickname "Pops" (because of the way he "popped cars off the track"). Turner was willing to do whatever it took to beat his on-track competition. His on-track performances quickly made him a series favorite, and *Sports Illustrated* called him the "Babe Ruth of stock car racing."

His off-track antics were just as noteworthy, and he and Little Joe Weatherly (another early NASCAR star) soon developed a reputation for closing bars and trashing rental cars (in impromptu driving competitions). By 1956, Turner had racked up 10 Grand National stock car victories and was one of the hottest drivers on the circuit. He began that season as a Ford team driver at the helm of the Schwam Motors Co. Ford Fairlane. Ford executives had taken a fancy to the sales-floor traffic generated by wins on the NASCAR circuit and had decided to get into factory-backed stock car competition in a big way during the mid–1950s. Part of the program was to recruit top series drivers like Turner, his pal Joe Weatherly, Ralph Moody, and Fireball Roberts to the Ford fold. That strategy quickly produced victories for the Dearborn-based auto maker. Unfortunately, it

Curtis Turner's "Purple Hog" 1956 Ford was more than a little stock. Check out the full factory glass and chrome trim, for example. Though stock, with Turner at the helm, the little Fairlane was far from sedate.

took Turner until September of the season to score his first 1956 Ford win. But what a win it was!

The track in question was Darlington, and then, as now, it was the toughest venue on the stock car circuit. Turner was no stranger to the "Lady in Black" and, in fact, had sat on the pole of the very first Southern 500 in 1950. When the NASCAR circus rolled into Darlington for the seventh annual running of the Southern 500, Turner was in the caravan and more than a little hungry for a win. During pre-race qualifying, he hot-footed his number 99 "Purple Hog" Ford to an 11th-place starting berth. Buck Baker sat on the pole for the 500 with a hot lap of 119 miles per hour that year, but didn't figure much in the outcome of the event.

Speedy Thompson and Tim Flock vied for the race's early lead, but by lap 33, Turner had carved his way through the pack to claim the first position. He led laps 33 through 35 and then reclaimed the top spot again from lap 39 through 95. After trading the lead with Fireball Roberts, Marvin Panch, and Jim Paschal at mid-race, Turner took over for good on lap 202. When the checkered flag fell on lap 364, Turner was the first car to cross the line. His nearest competitor, Speedy Thompson, was more than two full laps in arrears to Turner at the time.

Take off the hand-painted numbers and sponsorship logos, and Turner's Fairlane probably wouldn't have looked out of place in a shopping center parking lot. It was that stock. Note the narrow racing rubber that characterized mid-1950s-style stock car racing.

The car that Turner used to dominate the field that day began life as a regular-production Ford Fairlane on the River Rouge assembly line in Detroit. Built over a full frame that sported front coil springs and a leaf spring-suspended live axle differential, the car was disconcertingly stock by modern standards. A 230-horsepower 312-cubic-inch (ci) "Y"-block engine provided motorvation for Turner's win that day, and "Pops" translated those ponies to the always-treacherous Darlington tarmac with the help of a column-shifted three-speed manual transmission.

Turner took in the quickly passing trackside scenery from within the confines of a very stock control cabin. A stock factory bench seat and a set of war-surplus seat belts kept him behind the bus-sized steer-ing wheel and in front of a stock dash that had been outfitted with aftermarket gauges. A rudimentary roll cage provided a modicum of protection in the event of a wreck, and a hand-held fire extinguisher was close by if a fire broke out. Beyond that, the cockpit in Turner's car was pretty much bone stock. Truth be known, so was the rest of the Ford.

Turner's career in the NASCAR ranks continued until the 1960s (with time out for a "lifetime suspension" for union organizing against Bill France's wishes). He met an untimely death in 1970 when the plane he was piloting augured into a hillside in Pennsylvania. A replica of the Ford he drove to Southern 500 victory in 1956 today belongs to Gerald Lawrence of Lexington, New York.

The 312-cubic-inch "Y" block under the hood of the "Purple Hog" cranked out an advertised 230 horsepower, a pretty impressive figure for its day. When put to work navigating the superspeedway at Darlington, those ponies equaled top speeds near the 120 mark.

TECHNICAL INFORMATION

Wheelbase	115.5 inches
Weight	3,155 pounds
Front Suspension	Independent, "A" frames, coil springs, air bags, and twin shocks per wheel
Rear Suspension	Live-axle leaf springs and twin shocks per wheel
Brakes	Reinforced/shoes/ventilated drums
Engine	312-cubic-inch OHV, single-carburetor, 230-horsepower V-8
Transmission	Column-shifted, three-speed manual
Speed at Darlington	118.683 miles per hour

RICHARD PETTY'S 1960 PLYMOUTH

There once was a time—hard as it might be for NASCAR fans to recall—when Richard Petty was known only as Lee Petty's gangly young son. Back in the earliest days of Grand National stock car racing, it was the senior Petty who was one of the biggest stars on the fledgling "strictly stock" circuit. In fact, when the very first race was put on by the new race sanctioning organization, Lee Petty was there. Petty's borrowed number 38 Buick (which he had driven to the race track!) was running well in the premier 1949 event in Charlotte, until he flipped it three times in the first recorded wreck in NASCAR history.

Before long, Lee Petty's strong performance on the track—in a string of Plymouths, Dodges, and Oldsmobiles—made him one of the series' earliest stars. Working out of his Level Cross, North Carolina, shop and relying on help from his two young sons, Richard and Maurice, Petty went from race winner in 1950 to series driving champion in 1954. The elder Petty would ultimately go on to win three Grand National driving titles and a grand total of 54 Grand National victories.

In 1958, Lee Petty added another driver to his team, his first son Richard. The addition created one of the first multi-car efforts on the circuit (not to mention the high-roller Kiekhaefer Chrysler teams, which had dominated the sport in the mid-1950s).

Race number one for the future king of stock car racing was at a track in Toronto, Canada. Young Richard was just 21 years old that day, and his first racing mount was a number 142 Oldsmobile. It was not an auspicious beginning, however, as a close encounter with the retaining wall ended Petty's debut prematurely. He won just $115 for his 17th-place finish.

The purse for his second race, in Buffalo just 24 hours later, wasn't much more encouraging, since even though Petty finished this race, he got to pocket just $40 for his troubles. But better days were ahead for the youngster.

Win number one for Richard came in 1960 on dirt in a 100-mile race at the Charlotte fairgrounds. His racing mount that day was a 1959 Plymouth bearing the

Grand National stock cars actually were pretty darned stock back in 1960. Take the number 43 Plymouth that a young lad named Petty raced that season. Like most other cars on the tour, it started out as an assembly-line product, rather than a purpose-built racing machine.

Though Plymouth "wing" cars might not have shown up until 1970, there's no doubt that Plymouth "fin" cars were making hot laps long before then. Though strictly a creation of the styling studio, the fins on the back of Petty's 1960 Plymouth might actually have helped a bit in the corners.

now-familiar number 43. In the group of drivers he bested was another young fellow named David Pearson. It would not be the last time that Petty and Pearson would vie for a Grand National win.

Petty's first major win came in April of the same year when he won the Virginia 500 at Martinsville. By then he had switched to a Petty Blue 1960 Plymouth. He showed that car's soaring rear fins to many of the sport's best-known drivers that day, including Glenn Wood, Rex White, Joe Weatherly, Junior Johnson, Buck Baker, Freddie Lorenzen, and Ned Jarrett. Petty ultimately scored a total of three wins that season and 25 top-five finishes. That performance placed him second in the championship points race (behind winner Rex White) and earned him $41,872.

The 1960 Plymouth that claimed most of Petty's wins that year was, like all cars in the NASCAR ranks at the time, built from a regular-production automobile. In the case of Petty's Plymouth, the starting point was a base Savoy. It was a Homerically configured car and carried its 3,250-pound, 208.2-inch bulk over a 118-inch wheelbase. Decked out with tons of bright-work at the bow and a set of the exaggerated fins typ-

The interior of a 1960 Plymouth stock car wasn't all that far removed from, say, June Cleaver's grocery-getter. Check out the stock door panels, full roll-up glass, and mostly stock dash.

ical of the era, the two-door behemoth at first might seem a poor choice for a race car. But, actually, compared to most of the cars it was pitted against, Petty's car wasn't really at much of a disadvantage. Especially since it packed a 330-horse "high-block" 383 wedge motor under its block-long hood. The car's bulk and weight notwithstanding, speeds in excess of 142 miles

A high-deck engine provided the grunt for the 150-mile-per-hour racing speeds that characterized the Grand National tour in the early 1960s. Like the rest of Petty's Plymouth, that engine was decidedly stock. Note the absence of tube headers, for example. And the cast-iron low-rise-style single four-barrel intake is just about as "un-racy" as you can get.

Though it's hard to imagine, there once was a time when Richard Petty (that's the King of Stock Car Racing to you) was just an unknown kid. That time was the late 1950s and early 1960s. By 1963, though, he stepped out of the shadow of his father, Lee, and became a stock car star in his own right.

Mopar race cars throughout the 1960s and 1970s, like Petty's Plymouth, relied on torsion bars for front suspension movement. Note the reinforced shock towers that have been added to the engine bay in anticipation of race duty. If the single-reservoir master cylinder looks a little iffy in terms of ultimate stopping power, it probably was. But that was the nature of NASCAR racing in the early 1960s.

per hour were achievable at Daytona with the beast, and it's just possible that the Savoy's soaring rear fins aided stability in the corners.

In keeping with the "everything must be stock" theme of the 39-page-long Grand National 1960 rules book, Petty's Plymouth rolled on a beefed-up, but essentially unchanged, torsion bar/leaf spring suspension and double-centered 5-inch-wide steel rims. Drum brakes carrying fully metallic shoes and twin shocks at every corner were also part of the car's underpinnings.

The car's cosmetic package was also disconcertingly stock (especially when compared with the purpose-built "silhouette" cars that pass for stock on the Winston Cup circuit these days). Full safety glass was used all around, and the car even retained its window cranks and stock interior door panels. A single stock bucket seat was used to keep young Petty behind the bus-sized stock steering wheel and within reach of the column-mounted shifter. A NASCAR spec roll cage was installed, but compared to the jungle-gym affairs mandated by the rules today, it looked spindly indeed.

Other bits and pieces of the Plymouth's "ergonomic" package included a spring-loaded trap door carried in the left rear wheel well (used to check on tread life during a race), a package shelf-mounted brake light, and a handful of aftermarket gauges mounted in the essentially stock dash.

TECHNICAL INFORMATION

Wheelbase	118 inches
Weight	3,325 pounds
Front Suspension	Adjustable torsion bars, reinforced "A" frames, twin shocks per wheel
Rear Suspension	HD leaf springs, Chryco differential with floating hubs, twin shocks per wheel
Brakes	Reinforced shoes/ ventilated drums
Engine	383-cubic-inch OHV, 1-4V, 330-horsepower V-8
Transmission	Chrysler, column-shifted, three-speed manual
Speed at Darlington	125 miles per hour

Though Petty's Plymouth didn't look like a race car, that's just the purpose it served back in 1960. And quite successfully, too, we must hasten to add. The car pictured on these pages has recently been lovingly restored by Kim Haynes of Gastonia, North Carolina.

DAREL DIERINGER'S 1964 BILL STROPPE MERCURY

Truth be known, most auto enthusiasts don't naturally associate cars from Ford's Lincoln & Mercury division with racing and high-performance. Sensible (and perhaps even stodgy) cars are what folks often think of when the Mercury Man division is mentioned. But it wasn't always that way. In fact, on more than a few occasions in the past, cars of the Mercury persuasion have been the hottest mounts on the race track. And one of those times was the 1964 NASCAR season, when red, white, and blue Mercury Marauders were the class of the field.

Making that fact all the more remarkable was the location from which those cars came. Though one might have expected the Mercs in question to have been built at Holman & Moody's Charlotte shop, or at least somewhere else in the Deep South home of Grand National stock car racing, the 7-liter S-55 Marauders

we're referring to actually barked to life all the way across the continent in Bill Stroppe's Long Beach, California, race shop.

Starting with a body-in-white Marauder chassis, the Stroppe crew began its race prep with a complete tear down of all original components. With the frame exposed, the Stroppe crew then rewelded all of the original beads laid down at the factory. Special shock towers and brackets designed to accommodate two HD dampers per wheel were added. Next came the NASCAR-spec roll cage, which for 1965 carried quite a bit fewer bars than does a modern Cup car (for example, just one driver's-side bar was required by the rules).

Suspension components were addressed next. Heavy-duty front spindles served as the focus of the front suspension, and they were articulated to the chassis via boxed, gusseted, and re-engineered upper and lower con-

Though Bill Stroppe was based on the left coast, far from the heartland of Grand National stock car racing, his California shop still turned out some pretty mean race cars. And we mean both pretty and mean. The Marauders he built for Darel Dieringer were, without doubt, some of the prettiest stock cars ever built. They were also some of the fastest cars of their era.

Like other cars governed by the 1964 Grand National rules book, Dieringer's red, white, and blue Mercury was disconcertingly stock. Notice the car's stock bumpers and brightwork. The rest of the big Merc's cosmetic package was also essentially unchanged from assembly-line trim.

trol arms. A beefy sway bar was also installed along with short coils that carried a track-specific compression rating.

A heavy-duty, full-floater axle assembly was mounted at the rear, and incorporated hubs were designed to stay securely attached to the axle in the event of axle failure. Dual, track-specific leaf springs connected the differential to the chassis, and the whole package rolled on dual centered 5 1/2-inch-wide steel rims and 7 1/2-inch-wide treaded racing rubber. Huge 11x3-inch drum brakes derived from the Lincoln line were mounted all around and decreased speed somewhat under racing conditions.

Reinstallation of the mostly stock bodywork came next. In stark contrast to today's current crop of Cup cars, a stock car circa 1964 actually was pretty darn stock. Stroppe's Mercs even retained their factory roll-up door glass and hinges, for example. Interior work consisted of stripping out most of the car's original trim and then installing just the components needed for track work. In that number was a factory bucket seat that had been bol-

stered with extra padding designed to keep the driver behind the wheel in the twisties; a cast dash insert that carried a brace of aftermarket analog gauges; a taped-up and padded stock steering wheel; and an asbestos floor mat. A stock Ford floor shifter and a full safety harness rounded out the car's ergonomic appointments.

A non-fuel-cell-equipped, 22-gallon gas tank was mounted in the trunk and was secured with a set of additional hold-down straps. Quick-fill fuel inlets were still years in the future, so the tank was sealed off with a conventional twist-on cap.

When dressed for war in a fetching coat of red, white, and blue, one of Stroppe's Marauders stretched out over a 119-inch wheelbase and tipped the scales at a bit more than 2 tons. Power was provided by a high-performance version of the 427 big-block engine that Ford had introduced just one year before. Topped with a set of non-production (but race-legal—we didn't say the whole car was stock, did we?) High Riser FE head castings, and breathing through a sin-

A single production-based bucket seat was used to keep Dieringer (and his teammate Parnelli Jones) behind the stock steering wheel during a race. A cast dash insert was mounted just beyond that bus-sized tiller and was filled with aftermarket gauges. Save for the rather spindly looking roll cage of the day and the absence of a passenger-side bucket seat, the Merc's control cabin was stock in appearance.

A race-spec 427 engine was ready, willing, and able to punch Dieringer's Marauder through the air on command. That big block was based on the newly bored-out cross-bolted main-journaled FE engine that had been introduced just one year before. Topped with a set of race-only "High Riser" heads and equipped with a pair of free-flowing cast-iron "header-style" exhaust manifolds, that engine could be counted on for more than 500 ponies at full chat.

gle Holley four barrel and a set of free-flowing cast-iron header exhausts, the big engine cranked out more than 400 horsepower at approximately 7,000 rpm. At Daytona, that translated into speeds in the neighborhood of 175 miles per hour. Pretty impressive for a block-long race car with all of the aerodynamic assets of a barn door.

Darel Dieringer was one of Stroppe's team drivers during the 1964 season, and his first outing in the number 16 Merc came at Daytona in the 1964 500. He translated an 11th-place qualifying berth into a seventh-place finish and pocketed $2,000 in prize money for his trouble. All told, Dieringer made 27 starts in a Mercury that season (for both Stroppe's Marauder team

and Bud Moore's). In those starts he scored one win (at Augusta, Georgia) and 13 top-10 finishes.

Parnelli Jones campaigned Stroppe-prepped Marauders on the United States Auto Course (USAC) circuit and posted seven races including a triumph at Pike's Peak. Those wins and other top-five finishes earned Jones the USAC National driving title for 1964.

Unfortunately, Stroppe's hopes for more Mercury wins were scuttled by a Dearborn decision to drop factory funding for his (and other) Mercury efforts. The few cars that he built continued to be campaigned the following season (Parnelli Jones drove one at Riverside). But no more wins were forthcoming.

One of the red, white, and blue Mercurys driven by Dieringer for the Stroppe team in 1964 has been restored by Kim Haynes of Gastonia, North Carolina.

TECHNICAL INFORMATION

Wheelbase	119 inches
Weight	3,715 pounds
Front Suspension	Screw jack-adjustable, reinforced "A" frames and HD coils, twin shocks per wheel
Rear Suspension	HD leaf spring-mounted Ford differential with floating hubs, twin shocks per wheel
Brakes	Reinforced shoes/ventilated drums
Engine	427-cubic-inch OHV, 1-4V, 410-horsepower V-8
Transmission	Borg Warner, floor-shifted, four-speed manual
Speed at Darlington	136 miles per hour

Little Joe Weatherly was one of the best-loved drivers on the early Grand National circuit. He was also one of the best drivers—period. Weatherly had returned stateside from North Africa duty in the "Big One" (where he was nearly killed by a Nazi rifle round through the face) to take up the daredevil sport of motorcycle racing. When winning American Motorcyclist Association (AMA) national championships on the two-wheeled tour became passé, Little Joe plunged into four-wheeled competition in the modified ranks. He was an immediate success. In 1952, for example, Weatherly finished first in 49 of the 83 events he entered. He upped that winning number to 52 in 1953 and took home the NASCAR modified title.

Weatherly was soon offered a factory-backed ride on the premier Grand National tour, and in time, he came to the Holman & Moody operation as a team driver. He scored his first official Grand National victory at the helm of a 1958 Ford in August of that year. All told, Weatherly would score 25 stock car wins. But it is without doubt that the two back-to-back Grand National titles he won in 1962 and 1963 will always rank Weatherly as one of the all-time stock car racing greats.

Those seasons, Weatherly was paired with another World War II veteran named Bud Moore. A Spartanburg, South Carolina, native, Moore had made a name for himself first as a mechanic (he provided the mechanical muscle for Buck Baker's 1956 Grand National championship) before becoming a team owner. Moore and Weatherly began their partnership in 1961 and quickly found success. Weatherly drove Moore's number 8 Pontiacs into nine Grand National victory lanes that season, including stops at the Old Dominion 500 in Martinsville, the National 400 in Charlotte, and the Southeastern 500 in Bristol. Weatherly and Moore wound up fourth overall in the Grand National standings for 1961 and approached the new season with the hopes of improving that mark.

Weatherly got the new season off to a promising start with a win at Daytona in one of the traditional

Bud Moore had built Pontiacs for team driver Joe Weatherly until late in the 1963 season. When the famed Spartanburg, South Carolina, mechanic joined Fomoco's going thing to field a fleet of Mercury Marauders. Like the Pontiacs that preceded them, Little Joe's Mercs went racing in red-and-black number 8 livery.

The race cars that Bud Moore built have always been some of the nicest on the track. Proof of that fact in 1964 can be found in the cockpit of Weatherly's Marauder. Though stripped down for the purpose of racing, the Merc's control cabin was as nicely detailed as a show car.

twin qualifiers before the 500. He started his red number 8 Pontiac fourth in the main event and led the first lap. At race's end, Weatherly trailed race winner Fireball Roberts (in his famous Smokey Yunick-prepared number 22 Catalina) and a young kid from North Carolina named Petty across the stripe for a third-place finish.

Win number one for Weatherly and Moore came at Concord one week later in a 100-mile dirt track event at Concord Speedway. Just one week after that, Little Joe kept his right saddle shoe (that he was fond of wearing while racing back in those pre-Nomex days) flat on the floor at Weaverville on his way to a second straight win. Joe won again at Concord that season as well as at Augusta (twice), Savannah, Chattanooga, and Richmond. When not first across the stripe, Weatherly was often not far behind, and he recorded 39 top-five finishes (including his nine wins). That was good enough to land him his first Grand National title and $70,742 in purse money for 1962.

Weatherly and Moore no doubt approached the 1963 season with great expectations. Pontiac was still their corporate patron and Weatherly's driving abilities had not diminished in the least during the off-season (regardless of the "party-hearty" lifestyle that he and fellow racer/friend Curtis Turner led). Unfortunately, those expectations were upset by General Motors' decision to abruptly terminate all factory-backed motorsports competition just days before the Daytona 500. It seems that GM executives were more than a little concerned about anti-trust legislation (in those days GM was the world's largest car manufacturer) and were leery of creating too high of a profile with continued NASCAR wins. There was also the pesky problem of the AMA ban on factory motorsports that GM had engineered in 1957. Since GM was supposed to be following that ban, both formal and informal (back-door) sponsorship of racing activities would have to stop.

Though Weatherly and Moore began the season as a team, they weren't able to make every race on the circuit due to the Pontiac cutback. They did combine forces at the Daytona 500, where Weatherly drove Moore's number 8 Poncho to an eighth-place finish. But, by the very next race on the circuit, Weatherly was "bumming rides" from other car owners on the circuit. Along the way he drove Pontiacs for Fred

The engine under Weatherly's hood for 1964 was a high-revving iteration of Ford's High Riser 427 engine. When NASCAR officials "legalized" the not-yet-production 426 Hemi engine for GN use that year, they simultaneously threw Fomoco teams a "bone" by allowing them to use the equally race-only High Riser head castings. In peak tune, an HR FE cranked out in excess of 500 ponies.

Harb, Cliff Stewart, and Worth McMillon as well as for Moore. He also drove Plymouths for Petty Engineering at some events and Dodges for Wade Younts at others. Topping it all off were the races that Weatherly ran for Moore in the 1963 Mercury Marauders he started fielding in September of that year (after signing on with Fomoco for the first time, an association that has lasted until today).

While Weatherly's season may have been hectic, it was without a doubt a successful one. At the close of the 53-race season, Little Joe had scored three wins (Richmond, Darlington, and Hillsboro—all for Moore) and 17 other top-five finishes. When the points were tallied up, Weatherly had won his second-straight Grand National championship. At the time, Little Joe was only the third man in NASCAR history to achieve such a feat (the other two being Buck Baker and Lee Petty). It was a phenomenal success and one that suggested great things for 1964, when Moore's team would enjoy full Mercury sponsorship.

The first race of the 1964 season took place at Riverside Raceway in southern California, and Weatherly qualified 16th in his red-and-black number 8 Marauder. As the race progressed, he was running well, but 86 laps into the 185-lap affair, a puff of blue smoke was seen from beneath Weatherly's car just as it entered Riverside's treacherous turn six. A split-second later the car crashed heavily, driver's side first, into the retaining wall that was located just inches off the racing surface. As was his custom, Little Joe was not wearing a shoulder harness that day, and of course, window safety nets were still years in the future. As a result, his head

TECHNICAL INFORMATION

Wheelbase	119 inches
Weight	3,715 pounds
Front Suspension	Screw jack-adjustable, reinforced "A" frames and HD coils, twin shocks per wheel
Rear Suspension	HD leaf spring-mounted Ford differential with floating hubs, twin shocks per wheel
Brakes	Reinforced shoes/ ventilated drums
Engine	427-cubic-inch OHV, 1-4V, 410-horsepower V-8
Transmission	Borg Warner, floor-shifted, four-speed manual
Speed at Darlington	136 miles per hour

came in contact with the unrelenting concrete barrier, snuffing out his life in a heartbeat. It was a tragic end for the man that many called the "Clown Prince of Racing" due to his inveterate habit of playing practical jokes.

One of the 1964 Mercury Marauders that Bud Moore prepared for Joe Weatherly is on display in the Joe Weatherly stock car museum trackside at Darlington.

Once upon a time giants ruled the earth—and the superspeedways. That time was the early 1960s, and the giants were the block-long Grand National cars that hurtled around tracks on the NASCAR circuit every weekend. One of the largest cars in that number was the full-sized Ford Galaxie race car built at Holman & Moody's sprawling Charlotte, North Carolina, airport complex. The NASCAR world of 1965 was quite different than the one we know today. Factory sponsorship was the lifeblood of the sport. And full-sized cars in the fullest 1960s definition of the term were the order of the day. Especially in the Ford family of race cars.

Though Ford had gotten completely out of the racing business in 1957 (in response to the GM-inspired AMA ban on factory-backed sponsorship of automotive racing), by 1961 Holman & Moody was once again receiving full-factory funding and had been charged with the responsibility of securing Grand National victories for the Big Blue Oval. The chief architect of those race track triumphs was to be Ralph Moody, a New England racer of some repute and a mechanical genius of the first magnitude. As the "hands-on" racing half of

the H&M concern, Moody was literally responsible for changing the mechanical face of the Grand National series. For more than a decade and beyond, the mechanical innovations cooked up by Moody literally determined the way that NASCAR race cars were built.

The high-water mark for Moody's development of the Grand National race car was 1965. For that was the year he perfected the suspension geometry that would serve as the basis for just about every Fomoco and GM race car's chassis until well into the late 1980s. First and foremost of those engineering accomplishments was the perfection of the rear-steer 1965 Galaxie front suspension. Based on the factory stock suspension components that came installed under every dirigible-class Ford Galaxie street car, Moody massaged and tweaked each and every "stock" component until it was perfectly suited for the rigors of Grand National stock car racing. Re-engineered and rewelded control arms, wrist-thick spline-ended through-chassis roll bars, massive 3-inch-wide Lincoln-derived fully metallic drum brakes, and an indestructible, full-floater 9-inch rear differential were all part of the Ralph Moody program. Some of

Ford's block-long Galaxies used to be the cars to beat. Among them was Dick Hutcherson's gold-and-white, number 29 Holman & Moody-prepared 1965 Galaxie.

Hutch's Ford was powered by a 427 Medium Riser engine that was good for upward of 500 ponies in race trim. Unlike the High Riser 427s that had been used just one year before, an "MR" motor used head castings that were pretty much the same as those used on a street-going Galaxie. Note the special Holman & Moody air cleaner that channeled cold air from the cowl directly to the engine.

those components still see service today on the Winston Cup circuit in only slightly modified form.

A Ralph Moody-built Grand National stock car, such as the one that Midwesterner Dick Hutcherson drove in 1965, began life, like all stock cars of the day, as a regular-production assembly-line vehicle. Once in-house at H&M, the car was stripped down to its essential sub-components and then rebuilt with racing in mind. The stock Galaxie frame was rewelded for strength, then fitted with control arms that had also been rewelded for both strength and to achieve re-engineered geometry. Steel tube towers came next to serve as the mounting points for a quartet of HD shock absorbers, and along the way the chassis was fitted with a splined sway bar that was connected to the lower control arms with heim joints and special bolt-on arms.

A Holman & Moody-developed full-floater differential was installed at the rear and kept in place under the chassis via trailing arms and a fabricated Watts link. Two more pairs of shock absorbers were also mounted aft. In between the two suspension extremes, Moody installed a multi-tube roll cage that, while not as extensive as required by the rules today, still offered a large amount of driver safety. In keeping with the stock nature of the sport in 1965, doors retained roll-up safety glass, full regulator gear, and even their stock door hinges. The rest of the interior was disconcertingly stock, too, right down to the factory dash panel and floor shifter. The single bucket seat was another stock unit that was only slightly modified for racing with the addition of foam-wrapped driver locating tubes.

Power was produced by a single four-barrel evolution of the 427-cubic-inch FE engine that was introduced in 1963. For 1965, NASCAR officials outlawed

The roll cage required by the 1965 GN rules book was a much-less complicated affair than the jungle-gym affair found in a contemporary stocker. Just two low-mounted side bars were required, for example. The car also lacked the underhood cage loops common on the modern circuit. Hutch's car did have a few extras not found in or under a modern Cup car, like full roll-up safety glass windows and hinged doors. Cleaning up all that shattered glass after a shunt must have been a chore.

the special "High Riser" head castings they had allowed just the season before (as a sop to Ford racers incensed by a decision to "legalize" Chryco's equally non-production 426 Hemi engine). As a result, 427s for 1965 came factory equipped with what came to be called "Medium Riser" head castings. Power was still impressive and more than sufficient to propel a block-long, square-edged Galaxie to speeds in excess of 170 miles per hour on big tracks like Daytona.

A 1965 Galaxie was anything but aerodynamic. Big as a house and built with an upright grille that could have served double duty as a barn door, cars like Hutcherson's Galaxie relied more on brute force than a slippery shape to turn in good times around a NASCAR oval. Of course, when you have a 7-liter engine under the hood, why worry about aerodynamics in the first place!

Most of a 1965 H&M Galaxie's exterior sheet metal was also just the way it had come out of a UAW stamping press. Tough rear fender openings were slightly flared for ready access to the 7 1/4-inch period racing rubber during pit stops. In the case of Hutcherson's car, a flashy gold metallic-and-white paint scheme accentuated by number 29 racing livery was the last thing installed before the car rolled out the H&M door under the power of a 425-horsepower big-block engine.

In 1965, Hutcherson (one half of the Hutcherson-Pagan race car fabrication concern in Charlotte, North Carolina) used those ponies to compete in 52 of the 54

Virtually every stocker of the 1960s rolled on special double-centered stamped steel rims that had been developed by Holman & Moody. The 1965 rules book limited width to 8.5 inches. Racing rubber was treaded in 1965 and measured in at around 8 inches in width. *Daytona Speedway Archives*

Hutcherson continued on as a Ford driver until 1968, when he traded his driving gloves in for Holman & Moody crew duties at the head of David Pearson's Torino-based team. With Hutcherson's tutelage, Pearson won his second Grand National driving championship that season and backed it up with yet another in 1969. Soon after Holman & Moody closed its doors in 1972, Hutcherson helped start up the now famous Hutcherson-Pagan (H-P) fabrication shop just north of Charlotte. H-P today is one of the premier race car construction facilities in the country.

One of Dick Hutcherson's 1965 Galaxies has recently been restored by Kim Haynes of Gastonia, North Carolina.

Drum brakes were the industry standard in 1965, and they consisted of reinforced shoes, drilled production backing plates, and 11x3-inch drums. Though they were able to achieve some decrease in maximum velocity, they were a far cry from the manhole-cover-sized discs under a modern Cup car.

TECHNICAL INFORMATION

Wheelbase	119 inches
Weight	4,000 pounds
Front Suspension	Screw jack-adjustable, reinforced "A" frames and HD coils, twin shocks per wheel
Rear Suspension	Screw jack-adjustable HD coils and trailing arms, Ford 9-inch differential with floating hubs, twin shocks per wheel
Brakes	Reinforced shoes/ ventilated drums
Engine	427-cubic-inch OHV, 1-4V, 425-horsepower V-8
Transmission	Ford T&C, floor-shifted, four-speed manual
Speed at Darlington	137 miles per hour

races on the Grand National circuit. Of those starts, the amiable Iowan won nine and finished in the top five in 32. Win number one came on dirt at Greenville, South Carolina, in April. Hutch, as his friends called him, also scored short-track wins at Myrtle Beach, Nashville, Greenville, Maryville, Augusta, Moyock, Oxford, and Hillsborough. Though fame-generating wins at super-speedway events eluded Hutcherson that season, his points total at year's end ranked him second only to eventual Grand National champ Ned Jarrett. Along the way, Hutch pocketed $57,850.

Lady Luck can be fickle—nowhere is that truer than in the auto racing. Still there are seasons—certain golden seasons—where that vexing lass will take favor with one or another of the drivers on a given circuit. For Cale Yarborough, 1968 was one such season. Short in stature and long in determination, William Caleb Yarborough grew up just down the pike from the fabled oval superspeedway in Darlington, South Carolina. His first efforts on the Grand National circuit produced mixed results, and at times Yarborough and his family barely made enough from his racing to make ends meet. Things began to change for Cale in 1966, when he caught the eye of Ford's racing elite. A job pushing a broom at the Ford racing factory of Holman & Moody Inc. coupled with a number of yeoman driver finishes the season before produced a ride in

Banjo Matthews' factory-backed Galaxie for the 1966 Daytona 500. Cale made the most of the high-profile opportunity by qualifying eighth with Matthews' poppy red number 27 Ford before going on to a second-place finish in the race.

Later that year, Yarborough received a phone call from the Wood Brothers' race shop, located just across the state line in Stuart, Virginia. That call would ultimately prove to be the turning point in Yarborough's driving career, as by the end of the conversation, he was offered a ride in the Wood Brother team's red-and-white number 21 Fairlane. In 1967, the newly formed team tasted victory at both the Firecracker 400 in Daytona and the Atlanta 500. That early success for Yarborough and the Woods was just a hint of what was to come in 1968.

Cale Yarborough and LeeRoy Yarbrough, though unrelated, had a nearly identical ability to find the fast way around a NASCAR superspeedway. The fact that both were blessed with slippery fastback Cyclones made the velocities they both achieved in 1968 even faster.

Cale's second full season with the Woods began with a change of racing mounts. Following the Fomoco custom of major body changes every two years, 1968 saw the introduction of an entirely new Ford and Mercury intermediate unit body. Gone was the stubby, formal-roofed silhouette of the 1966–1967 Fairlane and Cyclone lines. In its place was a longer, lower, and significantly sleeker body that featured a radically sloping roof line that looked fast even while standing still. When the decision came down from Detroit to make the Wood Brothers a Mercury racing operation, the team began construction on a fleet of swoopy Cyclones that turned out to be the fastest cars on the circuit in 1968.

Unlike the modern Winston Cup cars that car owner Yarborough now fields on the NASCAR circuit, Cale's Grand National cars for 1968 did not begin their lives as just a floor full of sheet metal and bar stock. And that's because stock cars were actually a lot closer to stock in the late 1960s than they are today. Race car construction in those days commenced with the receipt of a bare metal "body in white" (so called because the raw sheet metal of the car's unit body looked white under fluorescent lighting) that had been "bucked" on a UAW assembly line. Upon receipt, the unit body's stock front suspension was sheared off at the firewall and replaced with a beefed-up frame section (or snout) derived from the 1965 Ford Galaxie line. The new snout was mated to the stock unit body via long rails that ran down inside the Cyclone's rocker panels.

Next came fabrication of the NASCAR-mandated roll cage and front loop assembly. Once the chassis had been formed, suspension components were bolted into place. At the bow, the Woods installed reworked (rewelded and reinforced) unequal-length "A" frames first used under 1965 Holman & Moody Fords. Four shocks, a wrist-thick through-the-frame sway bar, and short stout coil springs rounded out the front suspension. Higher-rate-than-stock leaf springs took up residence under the rear of the car and mated to a Holman & Moody-developed floating hub-equipped 9-inch differential. Three-inch-wide fully metallic drum brakes were mounted on Holman & Moody-developed "spiders" at all four corners.

In final trim, one of Cale's 1968 Cyclones rolled on double-centered H&M 15x9-inch steel rims and 10-inch-wide treaded Goodyear "stock car special" racing rubber. Total weight for the 115-inch wheelbase chassis was a rules-mandated 3,900 pounds. Power to move all of that mass was provided by a 427-cubic-inch version of the race-proven Ford 427 engine. For 1968, a Tunnel Port headed iteration of the 427 had NASCAR's full blessing—as did the dual Holley four-barrel carburetors that had been wrangled as a concession to Chrysler's 426 Hemi. Stainless steel tube headers flowed back from the engine and around the corporate "Top Loader" four-speed that was nestled behind the engine. Then, as

Mercury's new fastback Cyclone body style was an immediate success in NASCAR circles. One big reason was the line's radical roof line that flowed in a nearly unbroken arc from A-pillars to deck lid. Aerodynamically, it was light years ahead of just about everything else on the track (except its equally as slippery Torino cousins, of course). All Plymouth and Dodge drivers could do that year was hope that help would arrive soon in the form of a styling change. In more than a few ways, the 1968 wins scored by Mercury drivers such as Cale Yarborough were the first shots fired in the Aero Wars.

now, mufflers were not part of the Grand National program, so every one of the 450-plus ponies the engine cranked out at 7,000 rpm could be heard bellowing all the way around the track.

Yarborough's first appearance in the slippery new fastback number 21 Mercury came at the 1968 Daytona 500. Torrential rains washed out the traditional Twin 125 qualifiers that year, so few beyond Yarborough (and other Cyclone drivers such as LeeRoy Yarbrough, Mario Andretti, and Tiny Lund) knew just how formidable a racing machine the new Mercurys were. Any doubts about that fact were quickly dis-

Though Yarborough's 1968 Cyclone was capable of regular trips past the 190-mile-per-hour barrier, it was forced to rely on drum brakes to curb those speeds. Fully metallic pads and reinforced shoes were part of the program, as were conventional wheel cylinders and special Holman & Moody-developed backing plates. Massive 11x3-inch finned drums derived from the Lincoln line rounded out the package.

Cale's Mercury rode the high banks at Daytona on a combination of 1965 Galaxie and Cyclone underpinnings. Screw jack-adjusted coils and Galaxie control arms were mounted at the bow, while a 9-inch differential and parallel leaf springs brought up the rear. When set up for superspeedway work, those underpinnings created a rake that looked racy both on and off the track.

pelled as soon as the racing grid pulled off pit road. Yarborough proved his record-setting 189.222-mile-per-hour qualifying speed was no fluke by convincingly leading the first 12 circuits of the 2.5-mile super-speedway. So dominant was Yarborough's car that day that he was able to overcome a one-lap deficit (incurred early in the race due to ignition trouble) and come back to win the race. In what had to be a discouraging note for non-Cyclone drivers, Cale's closest competition all day was the similarly named, but unrelated, LeeRoy Yarbrough, who was at the wheel of his own Junior Johnson-prepped Mercury.

As things turned out, the rest of the 1968 season pretty much turned out to be the Cale and LeeRoy show, as both of those Mercury *pilotos* just about ran off and left the rest of the pack far behind. Cale's number 21 car, for example, visited victory lane no fewer than six times, winning at the Atlanta 500, the Virginia 500, the Firecracker 400, and the fabled Southern 500. For his part, LeeRoy notched wins at Trenton and Atlanta and coupled with Cale to produce a total of 27 top-five finishes for their respective teams. Yarborough posted winnings in excess of $138,000 that season, more than any other driver on the circuit, and catapulted himself into the front echelons of the sport.

One year later, Cale and the Woods received an all-new beak for their all-conquering Cyclones that transformed the cars into Cyclone Spoiler IIs. The new nose made the cars even faster than they had been in 1968, and when Boss 429 power was finally permitted by Big Bill France in March of 1969, the new Mercs were the fastest cars on the circuit. Sadly, none of Cale's 1968 or 1969 Wood Brothers Cyclones is known to have survived in its original form

TECHNICAL INFORMATION

Wheelbase	115–118 inches
Weight	3,900 pounds (minimum)
Front Suspension	Screw jack-adjustable, reinforced control arms (1965 Galaxie) and HD coils, twin shocks per wheel
Rear Suspension	HD, screw jack-adjustable leaf springs, Ford 9-inch differential with floating hubs, twin shocks per wheel
Brakes	Reinforced H&M shoes/ventilated drums
Engine	427-cubic-inch OHV, 1 or 2-4V, 550–600-horsepower V-8
Transmission	Ford T&C, floor-shifted, four-speed manual
Speed at Darlington	144 miles per hour

(though the Wood Brothers' 1971 Mercury currently on display at the Joe Weatherly Museum in Darlington appears to have been bodied as a 1968–1969 car at one time). As a result, all that remains of Cale's sterling 1968 season are a few faded newspaper clippings and a collection of photos—mostly taken in victory lane, of course!

BOBBY ALLISON'S 1969 DODGE DAYTONA

Bobby Allison has had a long and illustrious (and some-times tragic) racing career. Since cutting his racing teeth at the Opa Locka speedway near his (original) Miami, Florida, home, he has won 84 Grand National/Winston Cup races on the NASCAR circuit and one national driving title. Along the way he has been both a factory Dodge and a factory Ford driver as well as fielding a series of his own independently backed Dodges and Chevrolets.

He ranks as one of the winningest Holman & Moody team drivers, for example, but was also instrumental in reestablishing Chevrolet as a force in stock car racing with his wheel work for Junior Johnson in the Coca Cola Monte Carlo during the 1972 season. He also played a pivotal role in the American Motors Corporation's (AMC) brief stint in NASCAR racing during the mid-1970s and posted several Winston Cup wins in a red, white, and blue AMC Matador.

As oddly configured as that Matador might have been, perhaps the wildest car Allison ever campaigned during his driving career was the winged Dodge Daytona that he drove for Mario Rossi during the 1969 Grand National season.

Though Dodge drivers began the 1969 season full of optimism, they quickly found that their new Charger 500s were no match for Ford's equally new Torino Talladegas and Cyclone Spoiler IIs. Something had to be done—and *fast!* Tankers full of midnight oil were burnt on the effort that ultimately produced the Dodge Daytona.

This is a Ford 429 engine, put out by Ford Motor Company. It was developed and run in test programs but was disallowed by NASCAR before it ...peled in a race.

Allison's winged car was powered by a full-race version of Chryco's venerable 426-cubic-inch Hemi engine. Though limited by the 1969 NASCAR rules book to just one 1 11/16-inch-bore carburetor, the Hemi under Allison's hood cranked out nearly 600 horsepower. And that was enough to propel the car to speeds in excess of the double ton down the back stretch at Daytona.

As race fans will recall, 1969 was the first season of the two-year factory-backed "Aero Wars," and Allison was one of the warriors for the Dodge boys that season. Interestingly, it was not his first tenure as a factory-backed Dodge driver. His first such stint was back in 1967. When David Pearson decided to jump ship and sign with Ford (and Holman & Moody), young charger Allison (who had just won a short-track race at Savannah in a Chevrolet he had built himself) was given the keys to his first factory-backed ride in Cotton Owens' Charger. Nine races later he had scored the new team's first Grand National win at Birmingham. Unfortunately, Allison's tenure with the Owens team was brought to an abrupt end later that season by a misunderstanding about just what was supposed to happen on the weekends that team manager Owens elected not to race. That happened at a short-track event in Oxford, Maine. When Allison got wind of Owens' decision not to field a Dodge at that particular event, Allison felt free to run his own Chevrolet there, which he did—with great success. He won! Unfortunately, that made a few higher-ups at Dodge more than a little dyspeptic. So ended Allison's first turn at the wheel of a factory-backed Dodge.

As mentioned, Allison was recalled to the Dodge ranks in 1969. His first outing as a Dodge driver that season came in the Daytona 500, where he qualified a new-for-1969 Charger 500 in 40th for the big race. Unfortunately, the Hemi in that red-and-gold Mario Rossi-prepped car lasted no longer than the 45th lap, thus relegating Allison to a dismal 43rd-place finish. Things were different at Rockingham one month later, when Allison turned a 10th-place start into a second-place finish. In March, he scored the first Grand National victory by a Charger 500 when he bested the field at the Southeastern 500 at Bristol. He added a second win for the team with his victory at North Wilkesboro in the Gwyn-Staley Memorial 400. Allison won again at Richmond in the Capital City 250 in September, the last scheduled event before his Charger 500 grew a soaring rear-deck wing and a pointy proboscis to become a swoopy Dodge Daytona.

Though Allison and his fellow Dodge racers had held great hopes for the new Charger 500 at the beginning of the 1969 season, much to their dismay, Ford's new Torino Talladega had proven far superior on the

Florida native Bobby Allison was one of the charter members of the "Alabama Gang." That's a name he picked up on the rough-and-tumble modified circuit, where he and his brother Donnie scored many wins. Allison's greatest success came on the Grand National/Winston Cup circuit where his hard-charging driving style earned him a series of factory-backed rides in cars like this Mario Rossi-prepped Dodge Daytona.

superspeedways. Hopes again had soared when word leaked out about a radically redesigned variant of the 500 called the Daytona.

As history records, Allison's first chance to drive the all-new Aero Warrior was spoiled by a controversy about track conditions and tire quality just prior to the inaugural running of the Talladega 500 in September. When Richard Petty, president of the Professional Driver's Association, led drivers away from the track in protest, Allison was in the caravan of teams that boycotted the race.

As a result, Allison's first chance to field his new winged car on a superspeedway came a month later at Charlotte in the National 500. And he made the most of it. He qualified sixth for the race with his newly re-nosed Dodge, and by lap 98 had placed the car at the front of the pack. All told, he led the race a total of six times that day and ultimately finished second overall. Ironically, he was bested that day by baby brother Donnie Allison, who put his poppy red Torino Talladega across the finish line 6 seconds ahead of Bobby's number 22 Daytona. The race was the first full-fledged head-to-head meeting between the new winged Dodges and the long-nosed Fords they were designed to beat. Disappointedly for Allison and the Dodge boys, the Daytona still wasn't up to the task of taking down its Fomoco rivals. As things turned out, that remained the case on the superspeedways until the last race of the season at College Station, Texas. Allison did post one more "wingless" Charger 500 win at Macon in the Georgia 500, and his record for the season was five wins, $69,483 in winnings, and a 20th-place finish in the points standings.

Allison returned to the Rossi team for 1970 and had his chances of winged-car superspeedway wins significantly enhanced by Ford's off-season decision to slash its racing budget by a withering 75 percent. He started the season off with a third-place finish in one of the twin qualifiers prior to the Daytona 500, and that's exactly where he finished in the "main event" at Daytona that year. More top-five finishes followed until Allison scored his first winged-car win in the Atlanta 500. He scored a wingless Charger 500 win later that year in Bristol at the Volunteer 500 and a final non-wing-car win at the season finale in Virginia (at the Tidewater 300). At the end of the 1970 season, Allison ranked second in the points standings, and his three wins and 27 top-five finishes had earned him $149,745 in winnings.

As is chronicled elsewhere in this book, Allison left Dodge in 1971 when Chrysler's decision to cut its own racing budget put his ride in limbo. Later that year he signed on with Holman & Moody, and from there his career in the NASCAR ranks has stretched until today.

No documented examples of the Charger 500s and Charger Daytonas that Bobby Allison drove in 1969 and 1970 are known to exist.

TECHNICAL INFORMATION

Wheelbase	115–118 inches
Weight	3,800 pounds
Front Suspension	Adjustable torsion bars, reinforced "A" frames, twin shocks per wheel
Rear Suspension	HD leaf springs, Chryco differential with floating hubs, twin shocks per wheel
Brakes	Reinforced shoes/ ventilated drums
Engine	426-cubic-inch hemispherically chambered, 1-4V, 600–650-horsepower V-8
Transmission	Chrysler 833, floor-shifted, four-speed manual
Speed at Darlington	153.822 miles per hour

"It scares me just to look at it" is what Ford driving star David Pearson said when he first saw one of Dodge's new Charger Daytonas. And that's pretty much the reaction that Buddy Baker and the other Dodge drivers of the day wanted from Pearson and the other Fomoco drivers who'd been causing them so much grief for the past two seasons.

Ford had brought Mopar forces to heel with the introduction of a swoopy new intermediate for the 1968 Grand National season, and their new Talladegas and Spoiler IIs had pretty much mugged Dodge's Charger 500 race cars during the first two-thirds of the 1969 season. So the arrival of the newly homologated Charger Daytona in late 1969 had the same salutary effect on Dodge driver morale that a front-lines visit by Bob Hope's USO show might have had on the soldiers in Vietnam. Baker and his cronies had taken such a beating for so long that the arrival of the all-new Dodge just couldn't help but put them in a better frame of mind.

As built by Ray Nichels' Indiana race shop, a NASCAR-spec Daytona was based on a stock Charger unit body that had spent at least a little while on a Chryco assembly line. And keeping that essentially stock origin in mind, it comes as no surprise that the basic suspension components fitted to a Daytona's racing chassis had a lot in common with those under a street car of the same feather. Take, for example, the torsion bars that were used up front to provide for suspension movement. Mounted to a boxed and partially fabricated front frame section, those race strength bars acted on fabricated control arms and a quartet of heavy-duty shocks. Fully metallic drum

Baker relied on 426 cubic inches of race-ready Hemi engine for fast laps at Darlington, Daytona, and Talladega. The big iron under Baker's hood breathed cold air directly from a low-pressure area at the base of the car's windscreen. That ram-air induction was then led to a single 1 11/16-inch-bore Holley four-barrel carburetor that was mounted on a ram box-type intake. It was the perfect setup to keep the Hemi well fed at high rpms.

brakes were also a part of the front suspension program as were double-centered stamped steel 15x9-inch rims and 10-inch-wide racing rubber (which was still treaded in those days). A corporate 8 3/4-inch differential was installed beneath a Daytona's rear wing and fixed in place with the help of parallel leaf springs and another double set of shocks. As at the bow, beefy metallic drum brakes were used to slow the car for trips to victory lane.

Power was provided by a single carb-equipped version of the race-proven 426 Hemi engine, first unveiled during the 1964 NASCAR season. Ram air induction was provided by a fiberglass air box that

LEFT

During his lengthy career as a stock car driver, Buddy Baker earned a reputation as a superspeedway specialist and was the first stock car driver to break the 200-mile-per-hour barrier. That record was set during the factory-backed Aero Wars, when Baker was a Dodge factory driver. The cars he was assigned to drive were, without a doubt, the most radical Grand National stockers ever devised. Called Dodge Daytonas, the cars represented the ultimate in aerodynamic performance. *Mike Slade*

linked the carburetor with a low-pressure area just beneath the windshield. The solo Holley fuel mixer mounted to a ram air box intake manifold in super-speedway trim, and from there combustibles flowed south to provide motive force for the forged steel and aluminum reciprocating assembly. Once consumed, spent gases flowed out toward the ozone layer through stainless steel headers and 3-inch, unmuffled dump tubes. Along the way, upwards of 650 horsepower was churned out. A corporate four-speed box torque multiplied that power and then sent it back to a track specific set of gears—usually something around 3.23 for superspeedway work.

When installed in a properly set-up racing chassis, a race Hemi helped a Charger Daytona produce nearly 600 pounds of positive downforce at the rear and just about 200 pounds of ground-hugging weight at the nose. The result was superior stability in the corners and breathtaking straight-line speed.

Bobby Isaac put his poppy red number 71 Daytona on the pole of the first Talladega 500 with a speed of 196.386 miles per hour, for example. And just a few months later, Buddy Baker drove the Chrysler R&D Daytona to a 200.447-mile-per-hour lap of the

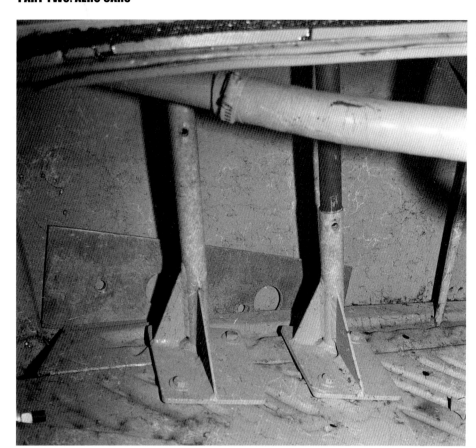

Special stanchions mounted in the trunk of Baker's car helped transmit the 600 pounds of downforce generated by the Daytona's signature wing to the tarmac. And that was enough traction-providing power to literally shred a set of Goodyear racing tires!

Buddy Baker became a popular commentator for a number of television networks.

same speedway. Baker's regular "ride" was the black-over-red number 6 Daytona that he campaigned for noted Chrysler team owner Cotton Owens.

Baker came to the Owens' team after a stint as Ray Fox's Charger driver the year before. Like the Fox "ride," Baker's day job for Owens was a fully factory-backed sponsorship. Though a drivers' strike denied the opportunity to draw first Daytona blood at the car's Talladega debut, he quickly put his new car's aerodynamics to good use at races following the Talladega 500. The next five races he and Owens entered in 1969 resulted in top-five finishes. Baker seemed poised to score the very first Daytona superspeedway win in the season finale at College Station, Texas, until a momentary lapse of concentration caused him to rear end James Hylton's car during a caution period.

More top-five finishes were in the offing for the day-glo number 6 car the following season, including a second-place finish in the Firecracker 400, a fourth in the Dixie 500, a sixth in the Yankee 600, a fifth in the Talladega 500, and a fifth in the American 500. The high point of Baker's 1970 winged-car season was, without a doubt, the convincing win he scored in the Southern 500 at Darlington. Baker qualified his Daytona second for the race (behind pole-sitter David Pearson's Talladega) and was always with the leaders in the race itself. He took the lead for the first time on lap 248 (of 367) and, for a time, diced with the Wood Brothers' Spoiler II driven by Cale Yarborough. Yarborough's crash on lap 331 opened the door for Baker's big red bullet, and he finished the race one lap ahead of his nearest challenger, Bobby Isaac, who was also driving a Daytona. The Southern 500 triumph was the third Grand National victory in Baker's career (he went on to score a total of 19 stock car wins) and the only time

TECHNICAL INFORMATION

Wheelbase	115–118 inches
Weight	3,800 pounds
Front Suspension	Adjustable torsion bars, reinforced "A" frames, twin shocks per wheel
Rear Suspension	HD leaf springs, Chryco differential with floating hubs, twin shocks per wheel
Brakes	Reinforced shoes/ ventilated drums
Engine	426-cubic-inch hemispherically chambered, 1-4V, 600–650-horsepower V-8
Transmission	Chrysler 833, floor-shifted, four-speed manual
Speed at Darlington	153.822 miles per hour

he mastered the Lady in Black at the fall classic.

One of the cars that Baker drove for Cotton Owens during the 1969 and 1970 seasons is currently on display at the Joe Weatherly Museum in Darlington, South Carolina. Outlawed by the whims of the NASCAR rules book in 1971, Daytonas like Baker's number 6 car still left an indelible mark on stock car racing. At the close of the two-season-long factory Aero Wars, Dodge Daytonas had won six superspeedway events (compared to six for Superbirds, eight for Spoiler IIs, and 14 for Talladegas).

The year 1968 was not a good one for Mopar drivers on the Grand National circuit. This was especially true for Dodge drivers who had hoped that their new "fuselage"-bodied Chargers would be able to manhandle their Ford and Mercury rivals. And truth be known, they probably would have done just that had Fomoco not "86ed" the boxy little Fairlane line during the off-season. The big problem for the Dodge boys was that the Fairlane's replacement turned out to be the slipperiest race car that had yet appeared in Grand National trim—and one that was far superior to the new Dodge Charger.

It was pretty obvious that something would have to be done to counter the new Fairlane and Montego menace—and fast. Returning to the drawing board, Dodge aerodynamicists redoubled their efforts to clean up the Charger's silhouette. The first item of business was eliminating the destabilizing lift created by the tunneled backlight that was part of the 1968 Charger's cosmetic package. While there was no way to duplicate the exaggerated fastback roof lines that made their Ford and Mercury rivals so fast, it was possible to significantly improve the Charger's own roof line by moving the back light upward to a position flush with the surrounding bodywork.

Once this rear window work was completed, the Dodge engineers directed their attention to the concave, air-grabbing grille design that had proven to be an aerodynamic handicap on race-spec 1968 Chargers. Following basically the same steps taken with the back light, engineers moved the stock Charger grille forward to a position flush with the front bodywork and then sealed it to the fenders, bumper, and hood with a rubber gasket. Airflow-smoothing A-pillar covers completed the

Chargin' Charlie Glotzbach was the driver for Ray Nichels' Dow Chemical team during the 1969 season. He stunned the racing world by nearly cracking the 200-mile-per-hour barrier during a "shakedown" run just prior to the inaugural race at Talladega in 1969. Unfortunately, he was robbed of the chance to translate that speed into a victory at the race because of a driver's strike. But it didn't stop his car from visiting victory lane!

THE WINNING CAR OF THE TALLADEGA 500 — SEPTEMBER 14, 1969

Though the win scored by the number 99 car at Talladega was sullied somewhat by the absence of most of the other top cars that were usually on the tour (and their being replaced by Grand American Mustangs, Camaros, and Javelins), it was still the first Grand National victory scored by a Chryco winged car.

aero makeover, and once done, Dodge engineers were more than a little pleased with their handiwork. So pleased, in fact, that they took the unusual step of unveiling their new creation—dubbed the Charger 500—well in advance of the 1969 NASCAR season.

It's likely that there wouldn't have been quite so much optimism in the Dodge camp had they known

about the new aero Fords and Mercurys that Ralph Moody and a crew of Ford engineers were working on at the same time. Ford's new aero-car (called the Torino Talladega) was ready and waiting for Dodge's new Charger 500s when Grand National teams pulled into the garage area at Daytona for Speedweek 1969. Much to Dodge drivers' dismay, they quickly learned

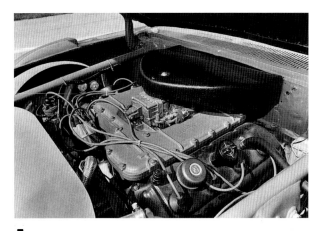

A full-race Hemi much like this one provided the grunt for Glotzbach's record-breaking 199-plus-mile-per-hour lap during qualifying at Talladega. Though that particular competition engine had been in service since 1964, it was still one of the most potent powerplants on the circuit in 1969, as Glotzbach's stunning speed indicated.

that their all-new race cars were still no match for Fomoco's even slipperier and equally new Aero Warriors. Worse yet was the fact that Richard Petty was so impressed with the new Ford race cars that he jumped ship during the off-season and was fielding Petty Blue Talladegas for 1969.

LeeRoy Yarbrough won the Daytona 500 in convincing fashion in his number 98 Talladega, and more Fomoco wins were quickly scored. Things got even bleaker for Mopar lovers everywhere in March when NASCAR, at long last, legalized Ford's version of the 7-liter Hemi race engine—the Boss 429. Adding insult to injury was the racing debut of that new engine in yet another Fomoco aero-car, the Mercury Cyclone Spoiler II. When Cale Yarborough used his Boss-powered II to whip all comers at the Atlanta 500, it was painfully clear that future Dodge victories would be highly unlikely unless something more was done to improve the aerodynamic performance of the Charger 500.

And so, it was back to the drawing board again. This time Dodge engineers pulled out all of the stops in their pursuit of superior aerodynamics. Directing their attention to the 500's still all-too-vertical (read: drag-inducing) grille, Chryco engineer Bob Roger and his crew cooked up an entirely new nose for their race car. Built around revised fenders and mounting a pointy nose cone that tapered down to a razor's edge, the new beak looked like it had come straight off some type of fighter jet down at the local Air Force base. Adding to that attack plane impression was the soaring rear wing that Roger's crew grafted on to the bustle of

the 500. Consisting of twin vertical airfoils that were connected by an inverted wing-shaped center panel, the new spoiler produced more than 600 pounds of positive downforce at speed. Working in concert with the 200 similar units of down pressure created by the new nose, the all-new car went through the corners as if it were on rails. In fact, it was quickly discovered that dialing in too much rear wing could generate enough downforce to shred the Goodyear rubber that race-spec cars rolled on.

Adding the new nose and wing to the rear window developed for the Charger 500 resulted in the Dodge Charger Daytona, one of the most radical cars to ever roll off an automotive assembly line anywhere in the world. Dodge scheduled the racing debut of the new car for the inaugural race at Bill France's new superspeedway in Talladega, Alabama, in September of 1969.

Dodge driver Chargin' Charlie Glotzbach threw down the racing gauntlet when he blistered the new track with a hot lap of 199.386 miles per hour in his purple number 99 Dow Chemical-sponsored Daytona. Trouble was, when Glotzbach was blistering the track, he was also blistering his tires. And so were all of the other drivers. It seems the new speeds made possible by the steeper-than-Daytona banking at Talladega, coupled with a very gritty track surface, made life very difficult for Goodyear and Firestone engineers. In fact, the tire compounds they had prepared for the first race at Talladega just weren't up to the task. So much so that leading drivers like Richard Petty, Cale Yarborough, and even Glotzbach himself began to have serious reservations about racing under the tire and track conditions that existed.

Tensions between the Professional Drivers' Association and NASCAR Chief Executive Bill France increased throughout the days leading up to the event. Threats and accusations were hurled like hand grenades from both sides of the issue until, ultimately, Petty loaded his Talladega up and left the track. Most of the other major drivers soon did likewise, leaving France with just a handful of independent racers left to "race." One of the cars that remained behind in the garage area was Glotzbach's fastest-qualifier Daytona. Though Glotzbach had followed Petty's lead and bowed out of the race, car owner Ray Nichels rounded up journeyman driver Richard Brickhouse as a replacement and announced to France that his team was ready to race.

When race day dawned, the sun climbed over the 33-degree banking at the track to reveal a motley assortment of Grand American Cars (NASCAR's "pony car" series of the day) and a handful of Grand

Though quick for their time, the gas stops turned in by Glotzbach's crew in 1969 were nowhere near as expeditious as those typical of modern competition. Part of the problem was the stock gas cap (seen dangling from a lanyard here) that had to be removed on every stop. Dry-break quick-fill gear was still years in the future.

National cars awaiting the green flag. When it finally fell, the race itself was run with a great number of tire-check cautions, and for the most part, cars on the track ran at speeds less than they were capable of for fear that an overstressed tire would come unglued without warning.

Three hours and 15 minutes after the race had begun, the checkered flag fell on the very first Talladega 500 with Richard Brickhouse in the lead. It was both his first and last win as a Grand National driver. It was also the first win scored by a Dodge winged car. Though garnered under less-than-ideal conditions and essentially without competition from the Ford and Mercury rivals the new aero-car was designed to beat, that first win still marked the arrival of the Daytona on the Grand National scene.

One of the few Dow Chemical Daytonas still in existence was recently located, and it was cloaked in later-model Charger sheet metal. It is currently awaiting a restoration to its wing-car plumage at the hands of Kim Haynes in Gastonia, North Carolina.

TECHNICAL INFORMATION

Wheelbase	115–118 inches
Weight	3,800 pounds
Front Suspension	Adjustable torsion bars, reinforced "A" frames, twin shocks per wheel
Rear Suspension	HD leaf springs, Chryco differential with floating hubs, twin shocks per wheel
Brakes	Reinforced shoes/ventilated drums
Engine	426-cubic-inch hemispherically chambered, 1-4V, 600–650-horsepower V-8
Transmission	Chrysler 833, floor-shifted, four-speed manual
Speed at Darlington	153.822 miles per hour

LeeRoy Yarbrough was a man with a clear vision of what he wanted to accomplish. He once said, "Some kids know when they're young that they want to be a doctor or a lawyer. But for as long as I can remember, all I wanted to be was a racer." And what a racer he was. After earning his "spurs" in NASCAR's rough-and-tumble modified ranks during the 1963 season, Yarbrough scored his first Grand National win at Savannah in May of 1964. LeeRoy rode into battle at that 100-mile dirt track contest at the helm of a 1963 Plymouth. He scored his second Plymouth win just six races later at Greenville, where he outpaced a young fellow named Richard Petty (also driving a Plymouth).

Superspeedway win number one for the Jacksonville, Florida, native came one year later at Charlotte in the National 500. Yet, even though Yarbrough was a proven winner on the circuit, he didn't immediately secure a full factory ride. As a result, his trips to the track continued to be sporadic throughout the 1967 season, when he fielded both Dodges and Mercurys (the latter for Bud Moore).

All of that changed in 1968 when Yarbrough signed on with Junior Johnson's factory-sponsored Mercury team. Of his decision to put Yarbrough in a

Though Ford's Lincoln Mercury division isn't automatically associated with motorsports by most NASCAR fans, in 1969 cars from the Mercury division were among the fastest on the track. LeeRoy Yarbrough drove long-nosed Cyclone Spoiler IIs for Junior Johnson that year and won just about every superspeedway race on the tour.

Yarbrough's Spoiler IIs had been designed for speed. Their special noses extended and lowered the car's normal silhouette to help it slip through the air with less resistance than a stock Cyclone.

number 26 team Mercury, Johnson said "LeeRoy's a charger and I like that. These drivers who lay back and save their equipment while waiting for the front runner to make mistakes or go out with mechanical trouble aren't my idea of real race drivers."

With that as a working definition, it's obvious that Yarbrough was about as "real" a race driver as Johnson could have imagined. Their pairing was an immediate success, and for the next three seasons Johnson and Yarbrough dominated the superspeedways and won more than $343,000 in the process.

Coupling Yarbrough's hard-charging driving style with the superior aerodynamics of a Johnson-prepped Mercury Cyclone proved to be a another successful formula. LeeRoy qualified his white-and-red car third for the 1968 Daytona 500 and then traded the lead with Cale Yarborough's Wood Brothers' Mercury for most of the race. Yarbrough led more than a quarter of the event's 200 laps and seemed destined to claim the checkered flag until Yarborough's number 21 car slipped past to claim the lead with just three laps to go. And that's the way the two cars ultimately crossed the stripe: nose-to-tail in first and second. LeeRoy and Cale went on to dominate the rest of the 1968 season. Yarbrough ultimately scored two wins and 15 top-five

finishes for his new team. It was but a taste of what 1969 would hold for Johnson and Yarbrough.

The number 98 Mercurys that the team's racing efforts were based around showed up at Daytona in 1969 with entirely new noses. Truth be known, those Mercurys actually showed up for the 500 as Fords! And that's because the new long-nosed Cyclone Spoiler IIs that the team would ultimately campaign were not homologated in time for the 1969 500. So, instead, Yarbrough drove a droop-snouted Torino Talladega in the race. Big Bill France also threw Fomoco teams for a loop by disallowing the Boss 429 Hemi engines that Ford had planned to unveil at Daytona. As a result, Yarbrough's Big T took the green flag powered by a 427 Tunnel Port engine (which, incidentally, had been built by a young Holman & Moody mechanic named Robert Yates). As things turned out, Yarbrough wasn't much handicapped by the sanctioning body's pre-race homologation shenanigans, and when the 500 was over, his Big T was parked in victory lane.

Both the swoopy new Spoiler II nose and the Boss 429 engine were finally allowed to race at Atlanta in March, and that new mechanical combination quickly proved to be a potent one. Yarbrough qualified his number 98 car eighth for the race, and

43

The control cabin in a race-spec Spoiler II was all business. It contained a single production-based bucket seat, a specially fabricated dash, and a roll cage nearly identical to the complex of tubes mandated by today's rules book. A production-based steering wheel, a factory shifter, and a brace of aftermarket gauges rounded out the ergonomic package.

Cale Yarborough, who was also back in a Cyclone at Atlanta, started fifth. LeeRoy's day was cut short by a troublesome transmission, but his similarly named (but unrelated) Mercury teammate did make the Spoiler II's first outing a winner.

LeeRoy's next start in a long-nosed Merc came at North Wilkesboro, where he came home second. He followed that up with a fourth at Martinsville before notching his first Mercury win at Darlington in the Rebel 400. He quickly reprised his role as a winning Mercury race car driver at Charlotte 15 days later, when he won the grueling 1969 World 600. Yarbrough qualified second for that 400-lap event and led from lap 162 all the way to the finish. When his white-and-red-

Though many might think that Chryco's winged cars were the ultimate superspeedway performers during the factory-backed Aero Wars, the NASCAR record book shows otherwise. When the dust had settled at the close of the 1970 season, Cyclone Spoiler IIs and Torino Talladegas had won a total of 22 superspeedway races compared to just 13 scored by winged cars.

trimmed Cyclone crossed the stripe, Yarbrough's nearest challenger was two full laps in his wake. It was an impressive performance. After the race Yarbrough said the 600 was "the easiest race I've ever won. After Richard (Petty) went out, Herb (Nab, his crew chief) told me to slow down. I cut it back to about 6,800 (rpms). It was almost a perfect day."

The Motor State 500 at Michigan was the next high-profile superspeedway race on the tour, and LeeRoy put his Merc on the front row with a qualifying run just a tick slower than pole-winner Donnie Allison's 160.135-mile-per-hour hot lap. When the green flag fell, Yarbrough showed the way back to the stripe and led the first 13 laps. He was also out in front at the end of the event and most likely would have claimed the win, except a last-lap tangle with fellow Mercury driver Yarborough put the number 98 car into the wall. Cale claimed the win, and LeeRoy ultimately scored fourth. As things turned out, it was to be the last drive in a Mercury for Johnson's team.

Though it was widely acknowledged that the Cyclone Spoiler II was superior to its Ford counterparts in terms of ultimate velocity, then, as now, Lincoln Mercury was not supposed to show up its parent Ford division. As a result, shortly after Michigan, the political decision was made to put LeeRoy back into a Talladega for the balance of the season (thus leaving Cale and the Wood Brothers as the only factory-backed Mercury team on the trail). As the NASCAR record book shows, that switch did little to slow the Johnson/Yarbrough juggernaut. Convincing wins at Daytona in the Firecracker 400, at Darlington in the Southern 500, and at Rockingham in the American 500 were just around the corner. Unfortunately for Mercury fans, those triumphs were added to the Ford win column.

None of the Mercurys or Fords that Yarbrough drove during his incredible 1969 season are known to have survived.

TECHNICAL INFORMATION

Wheelbase	115–118 inches
Weight	3,900 pounds (minimum)
Front Suspension	Screw jack-adjustable, reinforced control arms (1965 Galaxie or fully fabricated) and HD coils, twin shocks per wheel
Rear Suspension	HD screw jack-adjustable leaf springs, Ford 9-inch differential with floating hubs, twin shocks per wheel
Brakes	Reinforced H&M shoes/ventilated drums
Engine	Either 427-cubic-inch 1-4V, 550–600-horsepower (Tunnel Port/wedge head) V-8; or 429-cubic-inch 1-4V, wet-sump lubrication, 600–650-horsepower (Boss 429/hemi head) V-8
Transmission	Ford T&C, floor-shifted, four-speed manual
Speed at Darlington	151 miles per hour

"It's what's up front that counts." That's what a popular cigarette commercial of the day asserted (before the D.C. safetycrats banned all such broadcasts, that is). And while that claim may have been mere hyperbole as it pertained to cigarette construction circa 1969, it was more than a little meaningful when applied to the configuration of a Grand National stock car that same year.

Chryco sounded the "What's up front counts" theme first by introducing a race-modified version of the new 1968 Charger called the Charger 500. Ford forces countered with what came to be called the Torino Talladega at the Daytona 500 in February 1969. Both cars featured redesigned snouts that were intended to better slice through the wall of air that a racing car encounters at 180-plus miles per hour, speeds that had become common on the big tracks by the last half of the 1960s.

Early results of the "Aero Wars" were not encouraging for the Dodge boys, and at Daytona their new 500s were unable to keep the new long-nosed Fords out of victory lane—even though the sanctioning doges had denied Talladega teams Boss 429 Hemi power due to an alleged homologation deficiency. If the future looked bleak for Dodge and Plymouth drivers after Daytona, all hope must have been abandoned by them just one month later when Fomoco finally got the green light to race its all-new alloy-headed Hemi engine at the Atlanta 500. Ford and Mercury drivers had yearned for a race-hemi engine of their own ever since Chryco's 426 had been allowed out on the high banks in 1964. Ford's version of the hemispherically headed race engine featured huge, flapjack-sized valves, equally generous ports, and an all-new Ford-funded Holley "Dominator" carburetor that flowed more than 100 cubic feet per minute (cfm). Ford engine and foundry engineers bolted that impressive top end to a four-bolt main journal-equipped short block that featured a forged steel, cross-drilled crank, battleship-strength connecting rods that carried 1/2-inch rod bolts and, in a first for the NASCAR circuit, a dry-sump oiling system

When Cale Yarborough was a little boy he used to peek under the fence at the superspeedway in Darlington during races at that fabled track. By the late 1960s, that little boy had matured into one of the fastest drivers in Grand National racing. In 1968, he signed on to drive Mercury Cyclones for the Wood Brothers racing team. In 1969, those cars received special stretched-front sheet metal to become Spoiler IIs.

The nose work on a Cyclone Spoiler II was actually more aerodynamically efficient than the similarly configured beak on a Torino Talladega. The reason was the extra couple of degrees that were built into a Mercury's hood angle. Though seemingly insignificant, that extra angle translated into extra speed of nearly two miles per hour out on the track.

to ensure superior lubrication. In race trim, Ford's new big block churned out between 650 and 700 horsepower and could be relied on to do just that all day long (or for 500 miles—whichever came first).

Making matters even worse for Mopar fans was the fact that Fomoco also had an all-new Mercury intermediate race car to unveil at Atlanta along with the Boss 429 motor, and that new race car proved to be even faster (by 1 to 2 miles per hour!) than the sleek new Torino Talladegas that had given Chryco drivers fits at Daytona. Like the Talladega, the new Mercury menace was based on the fastback-roof lined intermediate body style that had been blooded during the 1968 Grand National season. Also like the Talladega, the new Merc mounted a stretched snout that both lowered and narrowed the car's frontal area. Mercury literature referred to the car as the Cyclone Spoiler II (named after a homologation run of spoiler-equipped street cars that came dressed in either Cale Yarborough or Dan Gurney livery). Not surprisingly, Cale Yarborough was one of the first Fomoco drivers to get his hands on one of the new long-nosed, Hemi-powered Cyclones, and the Wood Brothers dressed it up in their trademark red-and-white number 21 paint scheme for him at Atlanta.

Mercury PR types marked the event with a prerace parade lap consisting of dozens of street-going Spoiler IIs. Their presence on the track proved to be an omen for Yarborough and the Woods as the number 21 car quickly reclaimed the track for Mercury nearly as soon as the green flag fell. Cale put the number 21 car out front on lap three of the event and then went on to lead 308 of the race's 334 laps. At the checkered flag, Yarborough had 3 full seconds on the rest of the field for an easy win. After the race, the diminutive South Carolinian said, "This new Mercury and this new Boss 429 engine worked like clockwork." Clockwork indeed.

Test sessions with the new long-nosed Merc revealed that all things being equal, the car was 1 to 2 miles per hour faster than its Talladega stablemates on the big tracks like Daytona and Talladega. That difference was attributed to a subtle yet significant difference in the front fascia of both cars. Though a "T" and a "II" shared the same front bumper, grille, and headlight buckets, the slightly different hood line of the Cyclone line resulted in a header panel (connecting the cars' extended fenders ahead of the stock hood) that had a sharper angle of attack. That extra bit of inclination made a whale of a difference at speed. As a result, Cale's Spoiler II and the equally long-nosed Merc campaigned by LeeRoy Yarbrough for Junior Johnson were the fastest cars on the track. And that's just what Yarborough proved in June 1969 in Michigan, where he once again put his red-and-

In stark contrast to the 45-degree-angled "billboards" bolted to the back of the current Cup cars, the 1969 NASCAR rules book only permitted 1 1/2-inch-tall rear-deck spoilers on the back of Cale Yarborough's Cyclone Spoiler IIs. As it turned out, the car's basic shape was so aerodynamic in stock form that extra add-on spoilers and wings weren't really needed.

white race car in victory lane at the Motor State 500. He won the same race in a Spoiler II one year later, in 1970, along with wins scored in the same car at Daytona in a pre 500 qualifier and at the "Rock" in the American 500.

Similarly named but unrelated LeeRoy Yarbrough scored other Spoiler II wins at Charlotte in the 1969 World 600, at Darlington in the 1969 Rebel 400, at Charlotte in the 1969 World 600, and in the 1970 National 500 at Charlotte. So, you might ask, if Spoiler IIs were measurably faster than their Ford siblings, why didn't all Fomoco drivers switch to Mercury race cars? The answer, of course, was the interdivision politics that then (as now) relegated the Mercury division to

second-class citizen status within the Ford family of manufacturing divisions, as far as racing and promotional dollars were concerned. It is interesting to note that as soon as Ford folded its sponsorship tent in 1971, just about every Fomoco-based Grand National team quickly switched sheet metal to Cyclone trim—even after NASCAR effectively outlawed special aero-bodied race cars with a 5-liter engine rule for the 1971 season.

Though seemingly prevented from achieving its true place at the head of the pack by politics back at the home office, Mercury's Cyclone Spoiler II still played an important role in helping Fomoco win the Aero Wars that were waged during the 1969 and 1970 seasons. Though Dodge

TECHNICAL INFORMATION	
Wheelbase	115–118 inches
Weight	3,900 pounds (minimum)
Front Suspension	Screw jack-adjustable, reinforced control arms (1965 Galaxie or fully fabricated) and HD coils, twin shocks per wheel
Rear Suspension	HD screw jack-adjustable leaf springs, Ford 9-inch differential with floating hubs, twin shocks per wheel
Brakes	Reinforced H&M shoes/ventilated drums
Engine	Either 427-cubic-inch 1-4V, 550–600-horsepower V-8 (Tunnel Port/wedge head); or 429-cubic-inch 1-4V, wet-sump lubrication, 600–650-horsepower V-8 (Boss 429/hemi head)
Transmission	Ford T&C, floor-shifted, four-speed manual
Speed at Darlington	151 miles per hour

and Plymouth tried to counter the Talladega and Spoiler II juggernaut with radically winged and beaked race variants of their own (the Chrysler Daytona and the Plymouth Superbird), the final tally of superspeedway wins scored by both car makers during the two seasons showed Ford and Mercury drivers with 22 superspeedway wins to just 13 for their winged-car rivals. The Boss-powered IIs campaigned by Yarborough and the Wood Brothers in 1969 and 1970 played no small part in that dominance.

An exact replica of one of Cale's long-nosed Mercs has been restored by your author from a short-nosed Grand National chassis originally built by Tiger Tom Pistone during the 1971 season.

Announcers were fond of calling Benny Parsons the racing cab driver from Detroit. And, indeed, B.P. had spent a little time behind the wheel of a Motown checker. But dodging potholes in Dearborn did not turn out to be Parsons' life work. He was born to race.

Though many fans think of Parsons in terms of his 1973 Winston Cup Championship and the wins he scored in the 1970s and 1980s, Benny's first competitive laps around a Grand National (Winston Cup) oval actually came in 1964. Parsons was a promising Auto Racing Club of America (ARCA) driver on tracks around his then-Dearborn home base. As Benny's ARCA wins piled up, he came to the attention of Jacques Passino and other Ford racing executives.

Benny's first NASCAR race came as a direct result of that corporate interest. The race was the Western North Carolina 500 at Weaverville in August of 1964, and Ford assigned both Parsons and another series hopeful named Cale Yarborough to a pair of Holman & Moody-prepped factory Galaxies for what amounted to a Grand National "audition" of sorts. Parsons qualified his number 06 Ford ninth and finished 21st, when overheating sidelined the car near the half-way point.

Unfortunately, Benny was not "picked up" as a factory-backed driver after the race, and he returned to the ARCA ranks for a bit more seasoning.

But the powers at Ford still kept an eye on the lad from Ellerbe, North Carolina. In fact, it was a Holman & Moody-built Torino that Parsons picked up from Ford for the princely sum of just $1.00 that made it possible for Benny to cinch the 1968 ARCA national driver's championship. It's safe to say that Ford wasn't just feeling generous the day they offered the yellow number 88 Fairlane for a token sum. Ford expected good things to come from B.P. and was obviously investing in his future.

The folks in Dearborn's "glass house" made a similar investment in B.P.'s racing future by making him another good deal on an all-new long-nosed Torino Talladega (B.P.'s 1968 car having since been sold to Wendell Scott). As long-time NASCAR fans will recall, 1969 was the first year of all-out aerodynamic competition between the Fomoco- and Chryco-sponsored Grand National teams.

Yet, while those two halcyon NASCAR seasons are warmly remembered, the nearly identical battle for aero-supremacy that was simultaneously waged on the ARCA and USAC circuits is often forgotten. As you might have guessed, Parsons was one of Ford's "point men" in the ARCA Aero Wars. Benny's weapon that year was a yellow number 98 (and sometimes number 88) Torino Talladega. Like the other long-nosed Fairlanes that rolled out of the Holman & Moody race factory that season, B.P.'s Big T

During his active racing days, Benny Parsons was known as the former cab driver from Detroit. One thing is certain: He certainly knew how to "chauffeur" a race car around a NASCAR superspeedway.

Parsons was Ford's "man" in Automobile Racing Club of America (ARCA) circles, and he carried the corporate standard quite successfully, and in 1968 won the ARCA national championship with a fastback Torino. The long-nosed Talladegas he campaigned the next season made it two for two as Parsons won the ARCA title in 1969 also.

was built over a half-chassis pairing of 1965 Galaxie "snout" and rear Torino fastback unit body. Modified 1965 Galaxie suspension components were mounted to the reinforced big Ford frame member at the bow, and an H&M-perfected full-floater 9-inch differential working in unison with parallel leaf springs was mounted aft.

In between was the assortment of rectangular and round tubing that made up the car's side rail and roll cage assembly, a Spartan single-seat interior and a "full house" 427 Tunnel Port drivetrain. The whole package rolled on 15x9-inch stamped steel rims and a quartet of sticky Goodyear treated racing tires.

Like his Grand National counterparts, Parsons used his Talladega to bludgeon his ARCA rivals, and by the end

The rear suspension under Parsons' Talladega consisted of a full-floater 9-inch Ford differential, a pair of parallel leaf springs, and a quartet of heavy-duty shocks. Note the multiple-position front spring mounts and the cooling lines that led from the differential to the cooler.

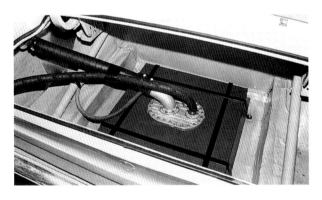

A NASCAR-regulated 22-gallon fuel cell was mounted in the trunk. It was housed on a sheet-metal "can" that was secured to the car with mild steel straps. Note the stock trunk hinges the 1969 rules book required.

of the 1969 season, he was once again that series' national champ. Along the way, he also drove the same car at a selected number of NASCAR events. First in that number was one of the qualifying races that preceded the 1969 Daytona 500. Parsons' hastily renumbered number 88 car (since LeeRoy Yarbrough had first dibs on the number 98 that Parsons used in ARCA events) started in the 11th spot at that race, and by the end of 50 laps was in fifth.

That performance in the qualifiers earned Parsons an 11th-place position on the starting grid for the 500. Though Parsons was never able to put the nose of his droop-snouted Ford out in front during the race, he rode around with the lead pack throughout the day and came home in seventh place (ahead of such series reg-

ulars as Richard Petty, Bobby Isaac, Bobby Allison, and Cale Yarborough).

Parsons' third outing in the Grand National ranks came at his "home" track on the Irish Hills of Michigan in the Yankee 600. Though Parsons' Talladega (now sporting the number 18) started the race in the fourth row (in seventh), on lap 150 a balky engine derailed that promising start, relegating him to a disappointing 38th-place finish. Things were decidedly different at the season finale in Texas. Though Parsons' 21st-place qualifying slot didn't promise much in the way of a top-10 finish, by the end of the Texas 500, he had worked his long-nosed Ford up to third place. It was his best result of the year and the ticket to a full series ride the following season in L.G. Dewitt's number 72 Talladega.

Benny kicked off the 1970 season with a 14th-place finish in the Daytona 500. At the end of his first full tour of the NASCAR circuit, he had turned in 12 top-five finishes (including a second in the Tidewater 300, a third in the World 600, a fourth in the Alabama 500, and a fifth in the Rebel 400). When the dust settled, Parsons was eighth overall in the season's points race and had pocketed $59,402 in prize money.

A replica of Parsons' 1969 Talladega has been built out of his 1968 ARCA Torino by Rich Turner in Orlando, Florida.

TECHNICAL INFORMATION

Wheelbase	115–118 inches
Weight	3,900 pounds (minimum)
Front Suspension	Screw jack-adjustable, reinforced control arms (1965 Galaxie or fully fabricated) and HD coils, twin shocks per wheel
Rear Suspension	HD screw jack-adjustable leaf springs, Ford 9-inch differential with floating hubs, twin shocks per wheel
Brakes	Reinforced H&M shoes/ventilated drums
Engine	Either 427-cubic-inch 1-4V, 550–600-horsepower V-8 (Tunnel Port/wedge head); or 429-cubic-inch 1-4V, wet-sump lubrication, 600–650-horsepower V-8 (Boss 429/hemi head)
Transmission	Ford T&C, floor-shifted, four-speed manual
Speed at Darlington	151 miles per hour

Back in the earliest days of Grand National stock car racing, the impact that aerodynamic forces exerted on a racing car was little appreciated. When more speed was needed, the simplest solution was to turn up the underhood thermostat a few degrees with a new cam, bigger carb, or larger engine. And that worked just fine for a time. By the early 1960s, the sanctioning body began to throttle back on a team's ability to generate horsepower by conjuring up all manner of performance-limiting rules. Engine size was set at 7 liters, for example, and restrictions were placed on carburetor apertures.

In time, top teams began to look around for non-engine-related ways to increase performance, and mechanics in a NASCAR garage area began to pay attention to the way their race car slipped through the air. Smokey Yunick was one of the earliest to work on aerodynamics, and many of his Hudsons and Chevrolets sported of add-ons and alterations that were designed to defeat the losses caused by drag.

Ralph Moody was another mechanical wizard in the NASCAR fold who devoted time to aerodynamics. As one half of the fabled Ford-backed Holman & Moody racing concern, Moody was ideally situated to influence both race car design and factory thinking. And that's just what he did in the fall of 1968.

The late 1960s found Fomoco and the Chrysler Corporation engaged in a take-no-prisoners battle for stock car supremacy. Both members of Detroit's Big Three were spending huge amounts of money in search of the superspeedway wins vital to sales-floor traffic on the Monday following a race. Both competitors had dedicated racing divisions to that task, and all manner of race-only hardware had been produced.

Dodge decided to up the ante in the factory-backed racing rivalry in 1968 by unveiling an all-new version of the Charger that had been developed specifically to cheat the wind on a NASCAR oval. The new car was

One of the secrets behind David Pearson's phenomenal success in 1969 was the extra 6 inches that had been grafted onto the nose of his number 17 Holman & Moody Torino Talladega during the off-season. Though far more subtle in appearance than, say, the radically pointed beak on a Dodge Daytona, the nose on a Talladega was actually quite effective. In fact, by the end of the Aero Wars, Ford Talladegas had beaten their Dodge and Plymouth counterparts on just about every NASCAR superspeedway.

Pearson's Talladega was powered by a full-race Boss 429 for most of the 1969 NASCAR season. That innovative engine consisted of a beefy four-bolt main-journaled block, cast-aluminum heads with full Hemi combustion chambers, and a battleship-strength reciprocating assembly. When properly tuned, a race Boss could crank out more than 650 horsepower.

called the Charger 500 (for obvious reasons) and featured a snout that had been aerodynamically slicked up by moving the grille forward to a position flush with surrounding bodywork. A special window plug was installed aft to "86" the lift-inducing "tunneled" back lights that came stock on regular Chargers that year. Rubber molding, molding used to seal grille work to sheet metal, and a set of airflow-smoothing A-pillar covers rounded out the new aero-variant package that was introduced at the fall Grand National race in Charlotte.

Unbeknownst to the Dodge boys, Ralph Moody had been hard at work on his own Aero Warrior just across town at the Charlotte airport-based Holman & Moody racing factory. Like his Mopar counterparts, Moody had lavished attention on the task of smoothing airflow over the bow of a Fomoco intermediate competition car. And like the Charger 500, Moody's ultimate design featured a grille made flush with its related bodywork. More than that, however, Moody had opted for the radical step of kicking out the whole nose section an extra 6 or so inches to a point that was both narrower and lower than on a stock Torino or Cyclone. A specially formed front bumper (that was made by cutting, sectioning, and rewelding a rear

The pit work turned in by Pearson's Holman & Moody crew was every bit as fast as his Talladega was on the track. By season's end, Pearson had parked his long-nosed Ford in 11 victory lanes and was the Grand National champion for the second straight season.

By the end of the two-season-long factory-backed Aero Wars in 1969 and 1970, Ford Talladegas and Mercury Spoiler IIs had racked up more superspeedway wins than any other cars on the circuit. The final tally of "mile or more" Grand National wins was 14 for Talladegas, 8 for Spoiler IIs, 7 for Plymouth Superbirds, and 6 for Dodge Daytonas.

bumper) and a special extra piece of bodywork that bolted home ahead of the hood (and between the newly extended fenders) completed Moody's design.

Ford engineers worked with Moody's design in a Michigan wind tunnel and found it to be a significant improvement over the flat-as-a-pancake, concave-grilled front sheet metal that was standard on every "regular" Fairlane and Montego. When working in concert with the already slippery bustle on a fastback Ford or Mercury intermediate's unit body, the all-new nose proved to be good for nearly 5 more miles per hour of terminal velocity—without any other changes being made to chassis or drivetrain. When you keep in mind that it takes an increase of about 15 horsepower to boost speed 1 mile per hour, you'll begin to appreciate how much of a success that new nose turned out to be.

Ford chose to bolt the new droopy snout on Torinos first, and scheduled the new variant's debut for the 1969 Daytona 500. When the Dodge boys arrived with their own new 500s, they were met by a squadron of the sleek new cars that Ford had elected to name after an all-new superspeedway then under construction in Talladega, Alabama.

Ford's other big news that day in Daytona was the planned racing debut of an all-new, alloy-headed hemi racing engine referred to variously as the "Blue Crescent," "Shotgun," and Boss 429. Unfortunately, Big Bill France scotched that idea by balking at the number of homologating engines that Ford foundries had (or, perhaps not) cranked out. And so Ford's new aero-variant went into battle with conventional wedge-headed engines under their bonnets for the 1969 500. But in the end it didn't matter. Holman & Moody driver and 1968 Grand National driving champion David Pearson signaled the supremacy of Ford's new aero design (even when powered by "last year's" Tunnel Port motor) by convincingly winning the first of the two qualifying races that preceded the 500. It wouldn't be the last time Pearson would visit victory lane that season. The 500 itself was won by Junior Johnson's driver, LeeRoy Yarbrough, who was also piloting a long-nosed Ford.

Pearson finished a respectable sixth in the 500 and visited victory lane for the second time in his blue-and-gold Ford just two weeks later at Rockingham in the Carolina 500. Win number three came one week after that at Augusta in the Cracker 200. All told, Pearson and his Talladega notched 11 wins in 1969, including victories at Michigan in the Yankee 500, Bristol in the Volunteer 500, and North Wilkesboro in the Wilkes 400. When not in front of the pack, Pearson's Boss 429-motorvated Ford wasn't far behind, and during the 52-race season, that duo scored an impressive 42 total top-five finishes. That was more than enough, as it turned out, to produce Pearson and Holman & Moody's second straight national championship.

In retrospect, Pearson's sterling season in 1969 was Ford's high-water mark in Grand National competition. A change in top-level management at the Dearborn "glass house" late in 1969 cut Ford's racing budget by 75 percent for 1970. Though Pearson stayed on with H&M and ultimately scored a Torino Talladega-based win in the Rebel 400 (at Darlington), without the full factory backing the team enjoyed in 1969, there was little that Pearson could do to combat the still fully backed Chryco competition.

Today, one of Pearson's all-conquering Talladegas has been returned to fighting trim by Kim Haynes of Gastonia, North Carolina, for noted muscle-car collector Floyd Garrett.

TECHNICAL INFORMATION

Wheelbase	115–118 inches
Weight	3,900 pounds (minimum)
Front Suspension	Screw jack-adjustable, reinforced control arms (1965 Galaxie or fully fabricated) and HD coils, twin shocks per wheel
Rear Suspension	HD screw jack-adjustable leaf springs, Ford 9-inch differential with floating hubs, twin shocks per wheel
Brakes	Reinforced H&M shoes/ventilated drums
Engine	Either 427-cubic-inch 1-4V, 550–600-horsepower V-8 (Tunnel Port/wedge head); or 429-cubic-inch 1-4V, wet-sump lubrication, 600–650-horsepower V-8 (Boss 429/hemi head)
Transmission	Ford T&C, floor-shifted, four-speed manual
Speed at Darlington	151 miles per hour

Mention the name Holman & Moody and what drivers come to mind? David Pearson? For sure. The two Grand National driving titles he earned while at the wheel of an H&M Torino make that association a natural one. And how about Fred Lorenzen? The number 28 Competition Proven Galaxies that Fast Freddie drove were, of course, Holman & Moody team cars.

But few folks automatically think of Bobby Allison when counting down the list of H&M drivers. Fact of the matter is, Allison was one of the winningest drivers to ever take an H&M car into battle.

Allison's tenure with the Charlotte-based team began in 1967. Though the Hueytown, Alabama, native had begun that season as a Dodge driver for the Cotton Owens team, by mid-season he and Owens had parted ways. In one of those rare coincidences that some call fate, Fred Lorenzen, Holman & Moody's team driver, had decided to retire from driving at about the same time. Though no longer in the driver's seat, Lorenzen still wanted to remain active in the sport, and that

desire led him to suggest the creation of an all-new Holman & Moody team, with Lorenzen as the team manager and David Pearson, who hopped into the seat vacated by Fast Freddie, as one of the drivers .

Just prior to the American 500 at Rockingham, Lorenzen got the formal OK for his project from the Ford racing brass. With that approval in hand, he set about looking for a driver. But according to Lorenzen at the time, that choice didn't require a lot of thought. Lorenzen said, "I got a call and was informed that I could have any car and driver I wanted for the American 500. I lined up the equipment I wanted, and I knew Bobby Allison would be my choice for driver . . . if I could get him." As already mentioned, Allison was available, and he and Lorenzen quickly came to terms on a contract.

The car that the 29-year-old Allison signed on to drive in the race was a number 11 Holman & Moody-prepared 1967 Ford Fairlane that was powered by a Tunnel Port 427 big-block engine. Jake Elder signed on as crew chief for the new team, and the new combina-

Though Bobby Allison is often associated with General Motors-based race cars, he actually ranks as one of the most successful Holman & Moody Fomoco drivers. As a matter of fact, Bobby actually drove for the "Competition Proven" team on two separate occasions. His most successful stint came in 1971, when he campaigned red-and-gold Coca Cola Cyclones for the team.

Ralph Moody fondly recalls the 1971 NASCAR season and considers the Mercurys he built for Bobby Allison as his favorite race cars. That's Moody with the "Blues Brothers" sunglasses, riding on the door of Allison's number 12 car on the way to victory lane. *Mike Slade*

tion clicked immediately. Though less than familiar with the handling characteristics of a Ford chassis, Allison was still able to qualify his little Fairlane third for the event, just behind a pair of Fairlanes driven by David Pearson and Jack Bowsher.

It was clear from the moment the green flag fell that Allison would be a factor in the race. He led the event six times for a total of 164 laps. When race leader Cale Yarborough dropped out with engine trouble on lap 389 (of 500), Allison took the lead for the final time and was able to hold off second-place finisher, Pearson, for the win. After the race Allison said, "From the first practice lap, I knew I had a car that I could win with. I had confidence in the car and complete confidence in Lorenzen's ability to run the team."

Allison took that confidence into the next (and last) race in the 1967 series, the Western North Carolina

500 at Weaverville, and won that event, too. Allison's performance in those two events garnered a factory-backed ride on the Bondy Long Ford for 1968, so his first tenure as an H&M driver was a brief but very successful one.

During the factory-sponsored Aero Wars in 1969 and 1970, Allison reprised his role as a Dodge driver and campaigned a winged Daytona dressed in red-and-gold number 22 racing livery. When the speeds generated by the special aero-cars raced those two seasons began to inch up toward the 200-mile-per-hour mark, the sanctioning body decided to slow things down by handicapping them for 1971 with a 5-liter engine limitation. That rule change effectively brought an end to the Aero Wars. As race fans of the era will well recall, the bottom was falling out of factory-backed sponsorship of the sport at about the

Allison relied on Boss 429 Hemi engines for power in 1971. Those monster engines could be counted on for something in the neighborhood of 650 horsepower in peak NASCAR tune.

same time that NASCAR was clamping down on speeds. And as a result, Allison's factory Dodge ride evaporated.

For a while he reverted to work as an independent driver and also did a little open-wheeled racing at a place called Indy. When a salary dispute resulted in David Pearson's departure from Holman & Moody just after the 1971 season started, Allison once again found himself at the helm of a "Competition Proven" car. In this case his competitive mount was a Boss 429-powered, 1969 "W"-nosed (or stock) Mercury Cyclone.

The first race of Allison's second stint as a Holman & Moody team driver was in May at Talladega in the Talladega 500. As with his earlier H&M work, Allison was successful almost as soon as he buckled up in the number 12 Coca Cola Cyclone. Race qualification placed the flashy car third on the starting grid, for example, and by lap six, Allison had rocketed to the front of the pack. His chief competitor for the lead that day was brother Donnie, piloting a Mercury for the Wood Brothers. After trading the lead back and forth throughout the event, it was younger brother Donnie who showed second-place Bobby the way across the

finish line. Even so, that second-place finish was just a hint of the success that was to come.

Race number two for Allison and the Holman & Moody team was the World 600 in Charlotte. There Allison translated a second-place qualifying start into a convincing, if grueling, win in the longest race on the circuit. Along the way he led the most laps (263 of 400) and averaged a then—record speed of 140.422 miles per hour. Following the race Allison said, "Getting this ride with Holman & Moody has to be the best thing that has ever happened to me. The pit work today was just excellent. I expect for some good things to happen the rest of the year." And indeed they did.

Win number two came less than a month later in the Mason-Dixon 500 at Dover. And Allison backed that up with yet another Holman & Moody superspeedway win in the Motor State 400 at Michigan. When H&M declined to enter a car at Riverside and Houston (the next two races on the tour), Allison drove his own Dodge to wins at both venues, making it five in a row for the Miami, Florida, native.

Allison was back in the H&M Cyclone saddle at Daytona for the Firecracker, where he started fifth and finished sixth. He followed that up with a second-place finish at Bristol, a third at Trenton, and a second at Atlanta before once again parking an H&M-sponsored car in victory lane at Winston-Salem. Interestingly, the car in question was an H&M-prepped Boss 302 Mustang and not his usual Cyclone! He drove that same Boss pony car to a second in the West Virginia 500 before resuming the Coca Cola Cyclone's winning ways with first-place finishes at both Michigan (in the Yankee 400) and Talladega (in the Talladega 500).

Allison qualified the Boss Mercury first for the Southern 500 at Darlington in September and went on to score his 28th career victory in convincing—and record (at 131.398 miles per hour average speed)—fashion. After the race Allison said, "I would say this is the best day I have ever had. Winning this race has to rank as one of my greatest thrills." One month later Allison thrilled the crowd again with an H&M win in the National 500 at Charlotte—his fourth straight superspeedway win that season.

Allison finished out his golden season with H&M with a win in the Georgia 500, a second place in the Capital City 500 at Richmond, and a third-place finish in the Texas 500 at College Station, Texas. When Ralph Moody was asked recently to pick his favorite of all competition cars he built and raced, he drove in 1971. It's easy to understand why.

Unfortunately, no examples of the Coca Cola Mercury are known to have survived.

TECHNICAL INFORMATION

Wheelbase	115–118 inches
Weight	3,900 pounds (minimum)
Front Suspension	Screw jack-adjustable, reinforced control arms (1965 Galaxie or fully fabricated) and HD coils, twin shocks per wheel
Rear Suspension	HD screw jack-adjustable leaf springs, Ford 9-inch differential with floating hubs, twin shocks per wheel
Brakes	Reinforced H&M shoes/ventilated drums
Engine	Either 427-cubic-inch 1-4V, 550–600-horsepower V-8 (Tunnel Port/wedge head); or 429-cubic-inch 1-4V, wet-sump lubrication, 600–650-horsepower V-8 (Boss 429/hemi head)
Transmission	Ford T&C, floor-shifted, four-speed manual
Speed at Darlington	151 miles per hour

Mention the words Grand National or, more recently Winston Cup, stock car and what type of vehicle comes to mind? One of Fast Freddie's H&M Galaxies? A winged Petty Superbird? A Darrell Waltrip Mountain Dew Buick? How about a Bill Elliott Thunderbird or a Dale Earnhardt Monte Carlo? You wouldn't automatically think of a Ford Mustang, would you? Yet there was a brief period when Mustangs, Cougars, Javelins, and Camaros did run with the "big dogs" on the Winston Cup/Grand National circuit.

The cars in question had all started out as contestants on NASCAR's Grand American (sometimes called Baby Grand) circuit in the late 1960s and early 1970s. But, for a number of races during the 1971 season, NASCAR actually let Baby Grand cars run against full-sized Winston Cup Cyclones, Road Runners, and Monte Carlos. And guess what—at least one regulation Winston Cup event was won by a Baby Grand Mustang. But we are getting ahead of ourselves.

As you might have guessed, NASCAR's Grand Touring and later Grand American division was designed to be an answer of sorts to the then-immensely popular SCCA-sponsored Trans-Am series. Like its SCCA counterpart, the Baby Grand division was comprised of American-built cars that roughly fell into the "pony car" category. Though the list of NASCAR-legal vehicles included Novas, Corvairs, Darts, Challengers, Mavericks, Falcons, Cougars, and Firebirds, the most-frequently campaigned cars were Mustangs, Camaros, and Javelins. The races these cars competed in were often

Better known for their success in the SCCA's Trans-Am series, Ford Mustangs also scored NASCAR victories in the Grand American division. One of the best-looking Mustangs to run in that class was Smokey Yunick's black-and-gold 1969 Boss 302. Though originally built to Trans-Am specs by Ford subcontractor Kar Kraft, Smokey converted the car for oval track use at Talladega.

Smokey's Boss was powered by a race-spec 302-cubic-inch engine. The little powerhouse was topped with two 1,050-cfm Holley Dominator carburetors when it first showed up at his Daytona Beach garage. Sustained high-rpm operation resulted in the production of more than 600 horsepower.

held in conjunction with a major Grand National event being put on the same weekend. In fact, the relationship between a Grand National and Grand American race was much the same as the current relationship between a Winston Cup and Grand National race today. The GA was sort of like the "undercard" race on Saturday before the "main event" on Sunday.

The cars that made up the GA division did not generally receive factory support and ofttimes were built in the racer's home shop. But that wasn't always the case. Take for example the Grand American Mustang that Smokey Yunick campaigned during the 1969 season. In point of fact, Smokey's beautiful black-and-gold Mustang was a highly sophisticated race car that had been built alongside Ford factory-backed Trans-Am Mustangs at Kar Kraft engineering in Michigan. Though first assembled with a 428 Cobra Jet Engine for power, once at the KK plant, the car was disassembled and fitted with a dual four-barrel-equipped Trans-Am Boss 302 engine. That engine was equipped with twin 1,050-cfm Holley Dominator carburetors and featured a beefy four-bolt bottom end that was capable of sustaining high-rpm operation. In race trim the little 302 was capable of cranking out nearly 650 horsepower—just

about the same as a race-ready big-block NASCAR Grand National engine of the same period.

In addition to the engine upgrade that Smokey's Boss received, the car was also fitted with a totally revised suspension setup. A full-floater differential was fitted, for example, and it was mounted to the chassis with the assistance of override traction bars and heavy-duty leaf springs. Massive Lincoln-derived disc brakes were also part of the car's rear suspension, as was a beefy rear sway bar. The Boss' stock unequal-length "A" frames were boxed and beefed for race duty and then reinstalled with reprogrammed steering geometry. Two more 12-inch discs and four-piston calipers were used at the front, along with another sway-fighting spring steel bar. Multi-adjustable Koni shocks completed the Boss's underpinnings.

Once completed, Smokey's Boss was sent south to his Daytona Beach shop dressed in a fetching set of gold "C" stripes and Yunick's signature black-and-gold racing livery. Once in-house, Smokey set about modifying the car for left-turn-only oval track duty in the GA division. The first things to go were the ever-so-fragile magnesium rims the car rolled on. In their place Smokey fitted a set of rules-mandated double-

Journeyman driver Bunkie Blackburn drove Smokey's number 13 Boss 302 at the inaugural Grand American race in Talladega. According to Smokey, the car was so fast that Blackburn was able to lap the entire field twice under green flag conditions. Unfortunately, an improperly heat-treated rocker arm derailed that effort, and the car was forced to drop out of the race. *Daytona Speedway Archives*

centered stamped steel rims. Interestingly, Smokey had to modify those rims with cooling scallops since the car came equipped with disc brakes (in an era when most NASCAR cars still relied on fully metallic drum brakes). Smokey also took the unusual step of mounting Australian Falcon steering components and a through-the-firewall reverse-wound starter motor in a search for more header room around the willing little 5-liter motor. Carburetion was also cut down to just one four-barrel fuel mixer, per the NASCAR rules book.

The car's first trip to a racing grid came in conjunction with the inaugural running of the Talladega 500 in Alabama. Ford's original plan was for Smokey to field his number 13 Talladega in the Grand National event scheduled for the Sunday of that racing weekend. When a controversy surrounding track and tire conditions resulted in a mass driver walkout, Smokey was told to ready the Boss for use in the GA race that was scheduled for the preceding Saturday. Smokey gave journeyman driver Bunkie Blackburn the nod to campaign the Boss, and he qualified the car high in the pack. During the race itself, as Yunick recalls today, Blackburn was able to lap the GA field twice under the green flag before an improperly heat-treated rocker arm (that Smokey still keeps as a memento today) failed, sidelining the car.

As mentioned, Smokey's Boss was far from the only Mustang to race in the GA division. Holman & Moody, for example, fielded a poppy red 1970 Boss 302 for both David Pearson and Bobby Allison during the 1970 and 1971 seasons. Surviving photos of that Rollins Leasing-sponsored car suggest that, unlike Yunick's Boss, the H&M Mustang was built in-house along "regular" Grand National (read Torino) lines.

And it was that very car that scored the one and only full Winston Cup series win for a Boss 302 in 1971. The race in question was the "Myers Brothers Memorial" held at Bowman Gray Stadium in Winston-Salem, North Carolina. In an effort to increase interest in the Grand American series and also improve the gate for the selected Grand National events, NASCAR combined the two divisions at select events on the circuit. The first of those was the afore-mentioned 250-lap event at Bowman Gray. NASCAR Vice President Lin Kuchler explained the decision to combine the two series was an attempt to benefit the fans by letting them see "the smaller car run against the Grand Nationals on the shorter tracks." He went on to say that the "record book shows the Grand American qualifying and race speeds are comparable to the Grand National speeds." Holman & Moody driver Bobby Allison proved as much by qualifying the number 49 H&M Boss 302 second for the event. The number-one qualifier was Richard Petty in a full-sized Grand National Hemi Road Runner. Allison explained his decision to drive the Mustang instead of his number 12 Boss 429 Cyclone by saying, "On tracks like this, we had the decided advantage because we could get in and out of the turns quicker."

And that's just what Allison did almost from the moment the green flag was shown to the field. Alli-

TECHNICAL INFORMATION

Wheelbase	110–112 inches
Weight	3,200 pounds
Front Suspension	Screw jack-adjustable, HD coils and reinforced control arms, twin shocks per wheel
Rear Suspension	HD leaf springs, Ford 9-inch differential with floating hubs, twin shocks per wheel
Brakes	Reinforced H&M shoes/ventilated drums
Engine	305-cubic-inch, single 4V, 500–550-horsepower V-8
Transmission	Ford T&C, floor-shifted, four-speed manual
Speed at Darlington	N/A

son took the lead from Petty for good on lap 113 and never looked back. After the event, second-place finisher Petty was not all that happy with the results. And he said as much. "I figured something like this would happen. They'll (the GA cars) probably win all these races. They ought to keep the two divisions separate. Grand National racing isn't supposed to be filled with Mustangs and Camaros."

Though little more than a forgotten footnote in the NASCAR record books today, Allison's victory in a Mustang that day in Winston-Salem is worth remembering. Though it never happened again (as the GA series was soon thereafter terminated), there once was a time when a Mustang showed Richard Petty's Hemi-powered Road Runner the way to the green flag. Smokey Yunick's Boss 302 today belongs to Pennsylvania's Ross Myers, while the whereabouts of Bobby Allison's H&M Boss is unknown.

Richard Petty delivered a wake-up call to folks in the Mayflower division late in 1968. Though he, like his father before him, had been a die-hard Plymouth adherent for more than a decade, Petty shocked the racing world by announcing his decision to campaign Fords for 1969.

So what was the reason for the "King" of stock car racing's decision? The answer was aerodynamics. Like all other NASCAR racers of the day, Petty had a pretty good appreciation of the role that aerodynamics played in race car performance. He probably had an even greater respect for the forces of aerodynamics,

Plymouth execs were more than a little embarrassed in 1969 when Mopar star Richard Petty jumped ship to drive a long-nosed Ford Talladega. Shortly after his departure, they resolved to find a way to lure the King back to Plymouth. The answer turned out to be the Plymouth Superbird. When Petty returned to the fold, he fielded Petty Blue winged cars for both himself and Pete Hamilton.

Hamilton's Superbird took flight with the help of a Petty Enterprises-prepped full-race 426 Hemi. The 600-plus ponies it cranked out produced speeds in excess of 194 miles per hour at Daytona in 1970. Note the ram-air-induction setup used to channel horsepower-rich cold air directly to the carburetor.

since the 1968 Plymouth Road Runner he had been assigned to race possessed all the wind-splitting abilities of your common brick. As a result, Ford and Mercury *pilotos*, blessed as they were with sleek, fastback-roof lined Torinos and Cyclones, pretty much had the measure of Petty and his Plymouth at every race track on the circuit.

Like other racers in the Chryco fold, Petty had gotten advance word on an all-new and much more aerodynamic Dodge Charger that was on tap for 1969. Petty wasted little time in putting his order in for one of those new race cars. Much to his chagrin, that request was rebuffed, and Petty was told that since he was a "Plymouth driver" he couldn't possibly race a Dodge race car. When all attempts to persuade his corporate patrons to reconsider their decision failed, Petty made a phone call to Ford racing chief Jacques Passino.

The purpose in Petty's call to the "enemy" was to see if he could persuade Ford execs to let him race one of the aerodynamically improved Torino Talladegas he had heard rumors about in the garage area. As it happens, Passino had been informally courting the "King" for a number of seasons. So when the phone call came from North Carolina the answer was an almost instantaneous

and enthusiastic *yes!* As the NASCAR record book shows, Petty's deal with Ford was quickly cut, and his familiar number 43 was soon gracing the side of a slippery Torino Talladega. Though he had never before campaigned a Fomoco chassis or tried to extract power from a Blue Oval racing engine, Petty was an immediate success that season. He began the year with his first-ever road course win in the Motor Trend 500 at Riverside, California. Nine other wins quickly followed, along with 31 top-10 finishes. By season's end, Petty was second only to eventual champion (and fellow Talladega *piloto*) David Pearson in the seasonal points race.

As you might imagine, Petty's defection did not sit well in Chrysler circles. The folks in the Plymouth racing division were particularly aggrieved at the loss of the "King"—to the point that they pulled out all the stops in developing an aerodynamically improved version of the boxy Belvedere body style, in hopes that such a car would lure Petty back to the fold.

Borrowing heavily from the same "playbook" that Bob Ropers' engineers used to develop the Dodge Daytona, Plymouth engineers began their Road Runner redo by first grafting on an entirely new nose cone. Adapted to the Belvedere unit body with the help of Coronet fenders and a hood extension, the new snout tapered down to a projectile-like point that was much more efficient at splitting the wind than the barn-door-like grille on a stock Road Runner. Also quite similar to the Daytona was the soaring three-element rear wing that the engineers bolted home on the new aero-variant's rear fenders. The twin vertical spars were airfoil-shaped in cross section and designed to provide superior lateral stability in the corners. The center wing section that ran between the uprights was also airfoil-shaped in profile, and its angle of attack was adjustable.

With its new nose, wing, and wind-smoothing A-pillar covers in place, the new Plymouth Superbird promised much better aerodynamic performance than Petty's old Road Runner. And that promise, along with the financial commitment to make Petty Enterprises the "Holman & Moody" of Chryco race car construction (meaning all future factory-backed race cars would roll out of Petty's shop), was what it took to persuade the King that his Ford fling was just a passing fancy. Soon ads in automotive publications all across the country were spreading the word of Petty's return. And that competition debut was scheduled for the Daytona 500 in February 1970.

When the Petty Enterprises truck rolled into the Big D's garage area that year, there were two Petty Blue Superbirds in tow. One carried the "King's" trademark number 43 racing livery, while the other car carried the number 40. The latter car was the mount of a young and promising rookie named Pete Hamilton. Blessed with good looks, thick blond hair, and more than a little driving talent, the young New Englander seemed destined to make his mark on the Grand National scene. That having been said, it's still likely that few expected much more than a respectable performance from the amiable young rookie in the 500 that year. But that's not how it turned out.

In qualifying, the Petty Enterprise 'Birds placed ninth and 11th on the grid, with Hamilton's number 40 car showing slightly better performance than Petty's Superbird. It was a harbinger of things to come. During the race both Hamilton and Petty ran well during the first handful of laps. Their new Aero Warriors were both fast and stable at the 190-plus-mile-per-hour speeds that characterized the 1970 500 field. Both cars looked to be strong contenders for the win until, without warning, the race-spec 426 Hemi in Petty's car let go in spectacular and smoky fashion. Soon the King was back in street clothes and providing color commentary for the Wide World of Sports race broadcast (which was tape-delayed in those days!).

With Petty on the sidelines, there seemed to be little hope left for a Superbird win in the 500. Indeed, the majority of the race was led by Dodge Daytona, Talladega, and Cyclone Spoiler II drivers. With 25 laps remaining, the race appeared to be David Pearson's to win, and the reigning Grand National champion's blue-and-gold H&M Talladega had a secure lead. Until lap 191, that is.

With Hamilton closing in with fresher rubber, Pearson momentarily got "loose" coming out of turn four and slid high. That was all the opportunity the number 40 needed to slip by, and on lap 192, Hamilton raced past the starter's stand to lead his second lap of the event. Try as he might, Pearson was unable to get past Hamilton's winged 'Bird, and when the flag fell, the number 40 car crossed the line three car lengths ahead of Pearson for the win.

Hamilton's win was a popular one. All the more so since no one (perhaps not even Hamilton himself) would have predicted it before the race. In April of 1970, he proved that his 500 win was no fluke when he finished first at the Alabama 500, the second race ever held in Talladega, Alabama (and the first "legitimate" non-boycotted race at that track). And when the circuit returned to Talladega for the second time in 1970, Hamilton proved he was the fastest man in the NASCAR ranks by winning the Talladega 500 in convincing fashion. Petty added 18 victories to the Plymouth win column in 1970.

Though seemingly filled with promise, Hamilton's Grand National career included just one more victory, that win coming in a Cotton Owens Plymouth at a 125-mile qualifying race for the 1971 Daytona 500. None of the Superbirds that Hamilton drove in 1970 are known to exist. Those in search of a winged Plymouth can visit the number 43 'Bird that is on display at the Richard Petty museum in Randleman, North Carolina.

TECHNICAL INFORMATION

Wheelbase	115–118 inches
Weight	3,800 pounds
Front Suspension	Adjustable torsion bars, reinforced "A" frames, twin shocks per wheel
Rear Suspension	HD leaf springs, Chryco differential with floating hubs, twin shocks per wheel
Brakes	Reinforced shoes/ ventilated drums
Engine	426-cubic-inch hemispherically chambered, 1-4V, 600–650-horsepower V-8
Transmission	Chrysler 833, floor-shifted, four-speed
Speed at Darlington	153 miles per hour

Fireball Roberts, Junior Johnson, Darrell Waltrip, Bobby Allison, Dale Earnhardt, Richard Petty, David Pearson, and Cale Yarborough: NASCAR stars all. And, without doubt, all fundamentally important to the success the sport enjoys today. But there were other drivers, many of whom most fans have never heard of, who were just as important to the development of Grand National—now Winston Cup—stock car racing. Who are they you ask? They were the independent drivers who, for years, made up the bulk of every race field. In the earliest days of the National Association for Stock Car Automobile Racing, there would have been no stock car races were it not for the participation of independent drivers. Even years later, when the three big auto makers were hemorrhaging sponsorship dollars at an alarming rate, independent drivers made up most of the show. Though few of them ever won a race,

without their presence in the starting grid, a NASCAR event would have been lightly attended indeed.

Cecil "Flash" Gordon was one of the journeyman racers who, for a time, made regular appearances on the Grand National and Winston Cup circuits. Gordon's name first began to show up on NASCAR Grand National starting lists at selected events in the late 1960s. By 1969, he was making sufficiently regular track appearances to finish the year toward the top of the points standings. Driving fastback Ford Torinos that year, for example, Gordon started all 51 events on the tour. By season's end, though, he had failed to win a single race and, in fact, had only scored one top-10 finish. However, Gordon had still amassed enough points to end the year with 10th place in the points race.

Gordon made 44 starts in 1970, scored two top-10 finishes, and came home 11th in the standings.

Cecil Gordon's ride during the early 1970s was this 1971-body-style Mercury Cyclone. Though seemingly about as aerodynamic as a brick, the car was actually quite slippery when it came to air management. Gordon relied on a Tunnel Port 427 engine to reach racing velocity.

Unlike the well-funded teams on the circuit who enjoyed Boss 429 power, frugal independent Gordon was forced to rely on a Tunnel Port 427 engine to make the field. Though long in the tooth as a racing engine by the dawn of the 1970s, Gordon's TP provided sufficient power to keep his car near the top of the points standings.

Gordon's best season on the Grand National trail was in 1971. He campaigned swoopy, fastback 1969 Mercury Cyclones dressed in yellow-and-blue racing livery. Of the 46 starts he made, he recorded six top-five finishes, the best a third in the Golden State 400 at Riverside, California. At year's end, Gordon was third overall in the championship quest, finishing behind series winner Richard Petty and runner-up James Hylton. Gordon won $69,282 in purse money that year and used some of the proceeds to upgrade his 1971 Cyclone. One of "Flash" Gordon's Mercurys is pictured on these pages.

Based on a Holman & Moody "half-chassis," Gordon's 1971 Cyclone featured 1965 Galaxie frame and suspension componentry from the firewall forward and a reinforced factory unit body from that point aft. Galaxie control arms and steering gear were bolted in place around screw jack-adjusted coil springs at the front of the number 24 car, while a full-floater 9-inch differential and parallel leaf springs were used to bring up the rear. Drum brakes measuring 11x3 inches were mounted all around to scrub off speed, and they acted directly on 15x9-inch double-centered steel rims and 10-inch-wide Goodyear racing rubber.

While the "big boys" on the 1972 circuit enjoyed the luxury of Hemi-powered rides (429s for Fords; 426s for Dodges and Plymouths), Gordon's more-modest budget only allowed years-old 427 FE components. A ram-air-fed single Holley Dominator bolted to the top of the Tunnel Port under the Cyclone's block-long hood and filled the TP's cavernous ports with Unocal racing gas on every rotation. A forged steel crank and cap screw rod-equipped "Lemans" rods were fitted to the beefy, cross-bolt, main-journaled block, and lubrication was provided by an integral dry-sump system.

As impressive as that technology might sound, it was years out of date by 1972. Still, Gordon made the most of what he had and turned in a number of respectable performances during the season.

The yellow Mercury made its first appearance for 1972 at the Winston Western 500 in Riverside, California, where it qualified 13th and finished 10th. Gordon's next top-10 finish came at Richmond (a ninth), and he followed it up with four top-five finishes (including a fourth at Martinsville) and 10 more top-10s. Though not a season marked by exuberant celebrations in victory lane, Gordon's performance in 1972 did garner him $73,126 in prize money and a fourth-place finish in the points race (behind Richard Petty, Bobby Allison, and James Hylton).

Gordon soldiered on as an independent for eight more seasons and usually finished each of those years in the top 10. In the 1980s, he opted to hang up his driving gloves and lend a hand to a couple of fellows named Childress and Earnhardt by becoming a key member of that all-conquering Chevrolet team.

Though never a "star" driver in terms of the number of races he won on the tour, Cecil Gordon was still an important part of the NASCAR scene during the 1960s and 1970s. One of the Cyclones he drove in 1972 has been restored by Alex Beam of Davidson, North Carolina.

TECHNICAL INFORMATION

Wheelbase	115–118 inches
Weight	3,800 pounds
Front Suspension	Screw jack-adjustable, reinforced control arms (1965 Galaxie or fully fabricated) and HD coils, twin shocks per wheel
Rear Suspension	HD screw jack-adjustable leaf springs, Ford 9-inch differential with floating hubs, twin shocks per wheel
Brakes	Reinforced shoes/ventilated drums
Engine	429-cubic-inch 1-4V, wet-sump lubrication, 600–650-horsepower V-8 (Boss 429/hemi head)
Transmission	Ford T&C, floor-shifted, four-speed manual
Speed at Darlington	153 miles per hour

His rivals called him "Jaws," he referred to himself as just plain "D.W.," and without a doubt, history will call him one of the best race car drivers of all time. His name is Darrell Waltrip, and he's a legend on the NASCAR circuit. But it wasn't always that way. Back in the late 1960s, D.W. was just one of many Grand National wannabes looking for a shot at the big time on the Grand National circuit. Waltrip had first taken to the track as a go-cart racer when he was a youngster in Owensboro, Kentucky. Later he had blooded himself in professional circles with three years of competition on NASCAR's sportsman division.

Along the way he had met and married the love of his life, Stevie, and they had pooled their efforts to further Darrell's career. In 1972, Waltrip took the first steps toward the 84 NASCAR victories he would ultimately score when, with the help of his father-in-law, an executive in the Terminal Transport Company, he acquired his first Winston Cup (nee Grand National) stock car. And what a car it was. Though it had been rebodied (a common practice then as now on the circuit) by the time he acquired the car, Waltrip's first big series mount had begun life in the Holman & Moody shop as a 1967 Ford Fairlane. Like other "half chassis" cars built by the fabled H&M concern from 1966

to 1971, the little Fairlane had started out as a bare unit body that had been welded up on a regular assembly line. Once at H&M, it had been fitted with what essentially was the race-prepped suspension from a 1965 full-sized Galaxie (front Galaxie frame member and all). Galaxie suspension components were used up front, and a leaf spring-mounted 9-inch differential was employed at the rear. A jungle gym's worth of roll cage tubing was also part of the race preparation process, as was a set of H&M-developed 3 inch-wide fully metallic drum brakes and a quartet of 15x8-inch reinforced steel rims.

As originally built, Waltrip's first Winston Cup car came powered by a 427 Tunnel Port engine and a Ford top-loader four-speed. As luck would have it, that very same car was the one assigned to Indy ace Mario Andretti for his "guest appearance" as a Ford driver at the 1967 Daytona 500. As raced, the car came painted in blue-and-gold racing livery and rolled on red-painted rims.

Though not a regular on the stock car circuit by any means, Andretti was a seasoned driver with a wealth of natural talent—talent that served him well whether mounted in an open wheeler or a full-bodied,

Darrell Waltrip was just a brash kid from Kentucky when he first showed up on the NASCAR scene. Outspoken and confident in his own abilities to the point of cockiness, he rubbed more than a few of NASCAR's old guard the wrong way—at least at first. Some of that first rubbing was done with the fenders on this 1971 Mercury Cyclone.

3,900-pound Grand National stock car. He proved as much by qualifying the Fairlane 12th for the 1967 500 and finishing a credible sixth in one of the race's two qualifiers. During the 500 itself, Andretti kept himself close to the front of the pack and out of trouble. To the surprise of many in the stands, the little blue-and-gold car took the lead on lap 23. After holding the lead on a number of other occasions, Andretti took the lead for keeps on lap 168 of the 200 making up the event. The only other car close enough to contest the lead was Ford teammate Fred Lorenzen, and once Fast Freddie became embroiled with Bud Moore driver Tiny Lund, Andretti had clear sailing to the checkered flag. It was Andretti's one and only NASCAR victory.

After its Fairlane service was over, Waltrip's first racer was upgraded to later-model Mercury sheet metal and ultimately wound up wearing 1970–1971 Mercury Cyclone sheet metal. And that's about the time that D.W. entered the picture.

Soon after acquiring the car, Waltrip had it repainted in Terminal Transport racing colors, a fetching combination of dark brown and tan. Though he would later be associated with the numbers 11 and 17, D.W.'s first Winston Cup car carried number 95 on roof, doors, and trunk. While updated to sleek Cyclone trim, things were actually little changed under the car's sheet metal from its first life as an H&M Fairlane. Which is to say that D.W.'s Merc still rolled around on what was essentially a 1965 Galaxie's underpinnings. One big difference was the motor under the lightweight hood. Though a full-house FE had once powered the car to victory lane, D.W. relied on an even-more-potent Boss 429 racing engine when he took the car out for his Winston Cup debut. As it turned out, that engine proved to be his undoing in that race.

The race in question was the Winston 500 at Talladega—the fastest race on the circuit in 1972. Bobby Isaac sat on the pole in the K&K Dodge Charger with a speed around the 2.66-mile track of 192.428 miles per hour. Waltrip's speed during qualification was somewhat more sedate and, in fact, only good enough to seat him 25th on the starting grid. Even so, Waltrip did start ahead of such NASCAR luminaries as Fred Lorenzen, Benny Parsons, and LeeRoy Yarbrough that day in Alabama.

Unfortunately for D.W., on lap 69, the Boss motor under his hood expired in a most dramatic fashion. His DNF placed him 38th in the finishing order and returned a princely $680 in prize money.

As you might have guessed, Waltrip was undaunted by the disappointing finish in his first race. More appearances on the circuit soon followed. And though they, too, often resulted in lackluster finishes, Waltrip pressed on. (The Mercury's next outing came at Talladega in August, where the motor only lasted until lap 99.) Waltrip's talents (while he was still run-

ning) began to catch the attention of car owners in the garage area. Of special interest to those interested observers was the surprising second-place finish D.W. scored at College Station, Texas, in the 1973 running of the Alamo 500. D.W. qualified his number 95 Mercury fourth that day, and though never in contention for the lead, he stayed out of trouble to finish just two laps behind race winner Richard Petty.

When Bobby Isaac suddenly retired in the middle of the August 1973 running of the Talladega 500 (that's right, Isaac pulled into the pits to announce his retirement to a, no doubt, stunned Bud Moore), team owner Moore asked the exciting new rookie to fill in for Isaac at selected races the rest of the season. It was Waltrip's first ride in a top flight car, and he quickly showed a return on Moore's investment by racing the number 15 Ford to an eighth-place finish in the 1973 Southern 500.

D.W. switched to Chevrolets for 1974, and the Mercury was retired. Many race cars since have carried his name—and often to victory circle. Even so, the sentimental driver never forgot his old race car. Recently he repurchased the car and had it returned to race-ready condition. Today the Terminal Transport Mercury is on display at D.W.'s race shop just south of the Charlotte Motor Speedway.

TECHNICAL INFORMATION

Wheelbase	115–118 inches
Weight	3,800 pounds
Front Suspension	Screw jack-adjustable, reinforced control arms (1965 Galaxie or fully fabricated) and HD coils, twin shocks per wheel
Rear Suspension	HD screw jack-adjustable leaf springs, Ford 9-inch differential with floating hubs, twin shocks per wheel
Brakes	Reinforced shoes/ ventilated drums
Engine	429-cubic-inch 1-4V, wet-sump lubrication, 600–650-horsepower V-8 (Boss 429/hemi head)
Transmission	Ford T&C, floor-shifted, four-speed manual
Speed at Darlington	153 miles per hour

PART THREE CHANGING TIMES

RED FARMER'S 1972 TORINO

Though Red Farmer's name is absent from the official NASCAR Winston Cup winner's list, he's been a fixture in the sport for many, many years. As race fans will recall, he was one of the first members of the "Alabama Gang," along with Bobby and Donnie Allison. Truth be known, none of that trio was from Alabama or even lived there when they first picked up their collective nickname.

As a matter of fact, all three were residents of sunny south Florida at the time. And all were hard-core modified racers who got their start at the Opa Locka speedway just north of Miami. When the local competition proved to be insufficiently rewarding (in terms of both skill and racing purses), Bobby, Donnie, and Red began to take their cars on the modified tour across the Southeast. Since the best races and biggest purses on the circuit in those days were all in Alabama, it was only natural that the trio spent a lot of time there. Over time, other racers forgot their south-Florida home base and began to associate them all exclusively with "the Heart of Dixie," Alabama. It was on one particular trip from Florida to a race in North Carolina that all three picked up their now-famous nickname. The setting for the naming was a feature event at a now-forgotten race track in the Tar Heel state. When Farmer pulled into the infield with the two Allisons in tow, one of the track regulars moaned, "Oh, no. There's the Alabama Gang." The name stuck, and the rest, as they say, is history.

In time, all three friends would relocate to Alabama and settle just outside Birmingham, which made their naming that night in North Carolina more than a little prophetic. The Alabama Gang's numbers also grew a bit after that relocation and ultimately came to include driver Neil Bonnett and Bobby's sons, Davey and Clifford (who both became drivers).

As mentioned, Farmer never went on to enjoy the same level of Grand National/Winston Cup success that Donnie and Bobby did. Instead, he was content to spend most of his racing time on the modified circuit, and he did enjoy many wins there. Even so, he did venture out onto the circuit at selected events, especially

Red Farmer was one of the original members of the Alabama Gang, and like his buddies Bobby and Donnie Allison, he'd gotten his start on the bull rings of the modified circuit. Unlike the Allisons, Farmer spent most of his career on these tracks. But he did make forays on the "big circuit" from time to time. He used this Torino in a number of early 1970s races at the Alabama International Speedway in Talladega, Alabama. *Mike Slade*

those that took place just down the road at Big Bill France's speed palace in Talladega, Alabama.

Today, one of the cars that Farmer campaigned at Talladega is on display trackside in the International Motorsports Hall of Fame. It was that particular gold-and-white number 97 Ford Torino that Farmer drove to his best Winston Cup finish at AIMS (Alabama International Motor Speedway), as the track at Talladega was officially called at that time.

The race in question was the 1972 iteration of the Talladega 500, and Farmer qualified his Ford in the 27th starting position for the event. The pole-sitter was Bobby Isaac's number 71 K&K Dodge Charger, with which he had cut a top qualifying lap of 109.677 miles per hour. The race was characterized by problems with a new version of the Goodyear racing tire. Though Goodyear was convinced that the new treaded rubber would be just the ticket for fast laps around the 2.66-mile superspeedway, there were problems lurking just below their sticky black surface.

One of the first to suffer was pole-sitter Isaac, who lost his shot at victory in a blown-tire-induced crash caused by Joe Frasson, who later said angrily, "These new tires Goodyear brought in here weren't worth a damn." His wreck took out a total of four cars and caused Richard Petty to spend 11 laps in the pits with suspension damage. The attrition rate was high for the rest of the event, especially for the top teams that had all purchased the new Goodyear shoes. All told, fully 32 of the 50 cars that rolled off the starting grid failed to finish.

As bad as the tire situation was for the hot dogs that day, it turned out to be a blessing for independent drivers like Farmer and race winner James Hylton. Since they didn't have the big bucks needed to buy the new race rubber introduced at the event, they rolled onto the track with "old style" racing tires. Once the race got under way, it quickly became apparent that the old Goodyear stock car specials were just as fast as the new tires, and they didn't suffer from the same durability problems (read: they didn't blow out as often).

At race's end, Hylton's Torino was the fastest car on the track and the only one besides Bud Moore's Ford (driven by Ramo Stott that day) still on the lead lap. Farmer brought his car home in fourth—eight laps behind the leader and just behind "Alabama Gang" member Bobby Allison, who was driving Junior Johnson's 1972 Monte Carlo.

Power for Farmer's top-five finish that day was provided by a race-prepared version of the cant-valved 351 Cleveland small-block engine. That high-revving power-plant provided motive for the car via a Top Loader four-speed and a 9-inch Ford differential. Coil springs and adjustable screw jacks provided the Ford-framed car with suspension travel, while quad shocks, a cross-frame sway bar, and a panhard rod kept that movement in check. Farmer took in the quickly passing AIMS scenery from within the safe confines of a NASCAR-mandated roll cage, and the security that structure provided made it possible for him to spend the $4,450 he won that day on something other than hospital bills.

Red Farmer is still a familiar sight at tracks across the Winston Cup circuit, and his mechanical advice is highly sought after by many of the series' newest drivers and crew chiefs.

Like modern Cup cars, the cockpit in Farmer's Ford was dominated by its multi-bar roll cage. Door glass and window regulators had been removed from the rules book by 1972, but a production-based bucket seat and steering wheel combo were still part of the competition picture that year.

TECHNICAL INFORMATION

Wheelbase	115–118 inches
Weight	3,800 pounds
Front Suspension	Screw jack-adjustable, reinforced control arms (1965 Galaxie and fully fabricated) and HD coils, twin shocks per wheel
Rear Suspension	Screw jack-adjustable HD coils, panhard rod, trailing arms, Ford 9-inch differential with floating hubs, twin shocks per wheel
Engine	351-cubic-inch 1-4V, 550–600-horsepower V-8 with wet-sump lubrication
Transmission	Ford T&C, floor-shifted, four-speed manual
Speed at Darlington	153 miles per hour
Speed at Riverside	110 miles per hour

When the fans began to file into the stands for the 1976 Daytona 500, they knew they were about to see some close racing. But it is doubtful that even the most imaginative in that throng would have been able to predict exactly how the race eventually turned out. And while it's certain that many fans that day expected tough, hard-fought racing from perennial favorites David Pearson and Richard Petty, the way those two arch-rivals would ultimately cross the finish line in the tri-oval area of the track in Daytona was simply beyond the ability of mere mortals (and probably even folks on the Psychic Friends hot line) to predict. It was, without a doubt, the most spectacular finish ever recorded in an automobile race, and one that brought the capacity crowd at Daytona, and the live TV viewing audience at home, jumping out of their seats. But more on that later.

The 1976 racing season dawned with David Pearson entering his fifth year as team driver for the fabled Wood Brothers racing operation based in Stewart, Virginia. Three-time Grand National champion Pearson had achieved early fame in the 1960s with championships scored in Cotton Owens Dodges and Holman & Moody Fairlanes. The year 1973 was even more successful for Pearson and the Woods, and by season's end their

Power for Pearson's 1976 Daytona triumph was provided by a Leonard Wood-prepped 351 Cleveland engine. Ford power parts were in short supply by 1976, so the Woods, like other Fomoco racers on the tour, were forced to make do with homemade parts and engine blocks shipped in from Australia. Even so, their number 21 team cars were often the fastest on the track.

red-and-white number 21 Cyclone had visited the winner's circle at an incredible 11 of the 18 races it had started. Pearson notched seven more superspeedway wins for the team in 1974 and two in 1975, and along

Not much can be said that's charitable about a mid-1970s Mercury's aerodynamics. Yet, when properly massaged (that's referred to as "cheated up" in the garage area), they actually won races. The Wood Brothers were especially adept at making a Mercury go fast. This particular car won the 1976 Daytona 500.

the way picked up the moniker "the Silver Fox." That name was based both on the fact that his curly black hair had gone to salt-and-pepper gray as well as on his practiced habit of lurking just behind the leaders until the waning laps of a race before showing his car's superiority.

The car that the Woods prepped for Pearson for the 1976 season was once again a familiar red-and-white number 21 Mercury. Though not as sleek as the Cyclones he had first driven for the team, Pearson's 1976 Montego was still no slouch, as his seventh-place qualifying position indicated. Like most other cars of the day, Pearson's car was built over a stock frame center section that had been augmented with fabricated front and rear tubular chassis "snouts." Fabricated suspension components derived from the 1965 Galaxie line were installed at the front, while a full-floater 9-inch Ford differential was mounted at the rear, in conjunction with long trailing arms adapted from a Chevrolet pickup truck. Stubby, high-rate coil springs allowed for at least some suspension movement at all four corners, while a quartet of shocks, front and rear, kept those gyrations safely in check. Disc brakes had found their way onto NASCAR race cars in 1973 thanks to Roger Penske's AMC Matador, and by 1975, the Wood Brothers had made the shift away from drum brakes, too.

Power for Pearson's 500 effort that year was provided by a full-house version of the 351 Cleveland engine. The sanctioning body had relegated big-block engines to the scrap heap with a series of ever more-restrictive carburetor rules, and by 1976 all teams on the NASCAR trail had elected to employ small-block engines for motorvation. With Ford on the sidelines in the 1970s, it was left to mechanical wizards like Leonard Wood and Bud Moore to cook up the high-performance parts necessary to kiss the "double ton" at Daytona and Talladega. Foremost of those components under Pearson's hood was a set of sliced and diced head castings that featured radically relocated exhaust ports. A ram-box-style intake topped by a single Holley carb kept the cant-valved iron heads fed, while a beefy "Australian" cylinder block and forged steel crank was used to brace the bottom end. External dry-sump oiling and tube headers dressed out the underhood area and did their part to help produce between 550 and 600 horsepower. That power met the pavement through a set of sticky Goodyear slicks that supported the 115-inch-wheelbase Mercury at all four corners.

As mentioned, Pearson qualified his Merc seventh for the starting grid at the 500, one back from Petty's day-glo red-and-Petty Blue Plymouth. When the green flag summoned the 42-car field to life that sunny February day, Pearson wasted little time in taking the lead—which he first assumed on lap five. Petty first put the nose of his Dodge out front on lap 57. By lap 100 it became clear to the fans in the packed grandstands that the 1976 500 would be yet another race that Petty and Pearson would divide up between themselves. The last 30 laps were all Pearson and Petty, with the Silver Fox leading 177 through 187, and

Petty slipping ahead from lap 188 through 199. The white flag fell over the two-car contest with Pearson tucked tightly in Petty's slipstream. That changed at the end of the Big D's backstretch when Pearson slingshotted past Petty to take the lead going into three. The King drifted high in the turn and seemed, for a moment, to be poised to return the favor to Pearson coming out of four. It was then, as both cars were running side by side at nearly 200 miles per hour, that Petty lost the handle on his number 43 Dodge. The two cars bounced into one another and then went madly careening into the wall and across the track with the checkered flag in sight. Petty's car kicked up a cloud of dust as it slid to a rest in the grassy area of the tri-oval ahead of Pearson and a mere 100 feet short of the finish line.

Unfortunately for Petty, the engine in his Dodge had stuttered to a stop during the melee. Pearson, on the other hand, though nearly blinded by a hood bent back and out of shape, was still under power when his car finally came to a stop some yards behind Petty's. While Petty futilely thumbed the start button on the dash of his crippled car, Pearson limped by him on the grass to take the checkered flag and the win. It would prove to be his first and only win in the Daytona 500. But what a spectacular win!

The car that Pearson limped across the line in that day has recently been lovingly restored by south Floridian Donny Gould. He uses the car today for shows and vintage racing.

TECHNICAL INFORMATION

Wheelbase	115 inches
Weight	3,700 pounds
Front Suspension	Screw jack-adjustable, HD coils and fully fabricated control arms, twin shocks per wheel, sway bar
Rear Suspension	Screw jack-adjustable, HD coils, panhard rod, trailing arms, Ford 9-inch differential with floating hubs, twin shocks per wheel
Brakes	Ventilated discs
Engine	358-cubic-inch 1-4V, 550–650-horsepower V-8
Transmission	Borg Warner Super T-10, floor-shifted, four-speed manual
Speed at Darlington	153 miles per hour

The more things change, the more they stay the same. And that's a truism that has cachet in a wide variety of settings, such as the racing world. Things tend to happen there in cyclical fashion. Take for example the widely reviled restrictor plates that currently afflict Winston Cup drivers on the fastest of NASCAR's superspeedways. Far from being new, they were actually first rolled out by the sanctioning body in response to the accelerated speeds produced during the factory-backed Aero Wars of the 1969 and 1970 seasons. Go figure.

The interest in aerodynamics displayed by teams on the Grand National circuit during those two sparkling seasons has also waned and waxed over the years in true cyclical fashion. Take for example the swoopy Chevrolet Laguna pictured on these pages. When it was raced in the mid-1970s, it was the slickest thing since . . . well since the Talladegas and Dodge Daytonas that had run in the same series in 1969 and 1970.

It seems that following the withdrawal of factory support for the Grand National circuit, stylists in

Chevrolet fans had little to cheer about during the 1960s, when GM got out of the motorsports sponsorship business. Junior Johnson changed all that in 1971 when he left the Ford ranks to field a Monte Carlo-based team. By the middle of the decade, Bow Tie race cars like Cale Yarborough's Laguna were the fastest on the track. *Mike Slade*

Detroit forgot all about the importance of aerodynamics. Or at least that's the conclusion one might draw by looking at the boxy, angular body styles that graced (blighted) salesroom floors during the 1970s. The race cars that resulted from that styling trend were, as a result, only mere shadows—aerodynamically—of the specially built factory aero-variants.

Though Chevrolet had officially been on the sidelines during the 1960s due to a self-imposed ban on factory-backed motorsports projects, Junior Johnson had brought that corporation back to the NASCAR fold (and the winner's circle) in 1971. The car he selected for that Bow Tie return was the first-generation Monte Carlo—a beautiful car to be sure, but not one that had been designed with aerodynamic performance in mind. Following the Monte Carlo, Johnson (and others of the increasing number of Bow Tie racers) switched to the Chevelle Malibu. Again, an attractive mode of transport, but one whose billboard-like grille and large side windows acted like an open parachute at racing speeds.

By the middle of the decade, the factory began to hear an increasing number of requests for an aerodynamic update for the Chevelle line. And though not openly involved in NASCAR competition (the back door at Charlotte had remained open even during the 1960s), GM was aware of the sales help that NASCAR wins provided. And so it was that Chevrolet decided to build the Chevelle Laguna S-3.

Based on the by-then-familiar Chevelle body style, a 1975 Laguna sported a unique front fascia that had been specifically designed to more efficiently slice through the wind. The new front fascia was much more severely sloped than the vertical grille design it replaced, and instead of a separate box-like chrome bumper, the new nose piece was all one unit with no visible bumper save for a rub strip. When dressed up in race trim with angled headlight block-off plates and a thickly screened-over grille opening, the new proboscis worked as a first-class airfoil by shoveling up air at track level and then directing it back over the hood and roof line.

Other important parts of the Laguna package were the skinned-over rear side windows. Whereas the stock Malibu body featured thin B- and C-pillars surrounding large glass house areas, on the Laguna these are trapping openings that were covered over in large part and punctuated only by a pair of "opera" windows (which themselves were mostly covered by slatted fascias). The overall result was a significantly slicked-up body style that was much more suited to high-banks work.

Junior Johnson today fondly recalls the number 11 Lagunas he fielded for Cale Yarborough during the 1975, 1976, and 1977 seasons. According to Junior, the cars were "really the start of all the current aerodynamic stuff going on nowadays." Of the Laguna's introduction, Junior offers that, "We'd been doing pretty good with the Chevy on the short- and mid-sized

tracks, but the Dodges and Mercurys were better than us at the faster speedways. We did a lot of testing at Talladega getting the Laguna refined. And it was the first real extensive effort at developing a sleek street version that we could race."

Though Johnson's reminiscences obviously overlook the all-conquering Talladegas that he himself had built for LeeRoy Yarbrough six years before, it's easy to understand his affection for the Laguna since it was, after all, the key to his first two Winston Cup championships as a car owner.

The first of those Laguna crowns was won by Cale Yarborough in the car that's pictured on these pages. Built over a Banjo Matthews-prepared chassis, the car was campaigned in yellow-and-white Holley Farms racing livery. Just below the surface was a mix and match of components typical of the Winston Cup cars raced during the mid-1970s. As mentioned, the frame was a creation of Banjo Matthews' now-legendary race car fabrication shop in Asheville, North Carolina. Welded up from differing lengths of round and rectangular tubing, the frame consisted of a central roll cage and a pair of front and rear suspension locating snouts.

An updated version of the rear-steer front suspension setup first perfected on Ralph Moody-built 1965 Galaxies was fitted at the bow. Boxed Galaxie lower control arms worked in conjunction with fabricated uppers and screw jack-adjustable coil springs. Dual shocks were mounted at each corner and a manual Galaxie box was used to dial in steering inputs. Chevrolet truck line-derived trailing arms and a Holman & Moody-perfected Ford differential served as the focus of the rear suspension. Another set of screw jack-adjusted coils allowed for suspension travel while another set of dual shocks and a cross-chassis panhard rod were used to keep that movement in check.

Reflecting the change away from drum brakes that had taken place in the Winston Cup garage area in the early 1970s, Johnson's Laguna was fitted with massive ventilated discs at all four corners. Slotted (for brake cooling) steel rims carried Goodyear racing slicks to make the chassis a roller.

A race-prepped version of Chevrolet's venerable small-block engine provided the motive force for Yarborough's first championship season. Built around a beefy four-bolt block and plumbed with a single four-barrel top end, an external dry-sump system, and a set of stainless steel headers, the willing little 5.8-liter engine produced between 500 and 600 horsepower in race trim. That was more than enough power to propel the number 11 car around tracks like Daytona and Talladega at speeds in excess of 180 miles per hour.

Yarborough's first outing in the Laguna pictured here came at the 1976 500 in Daytona. After qualifying the car a credible 14th, disaster struck on the very first lap when engine failure caused the car to DNF. It's likely

One of the reasons Cale's Holly Farms S-3 was so fast was the special nose piece it carried into battle. Formed from flexible plastic and angled to kick onrushing air up and over the rest of the car with a minimum of drag, the special Laguna nose was an invaluable aerodynamic asset to Cale and the Junior Johnson team. *Mike Slade*

that Cale would not have been inclined to predict a championship-winning season after his last-place finish in the 500, but that's just what happened.

Win number one for the team came at Bristol in March at the Southeastern 400. Yarborough backed up that victory with checkered flags at North Wilkesboro, Nashville, Daytona (in the Firecracker), Dover, and Martinsville as well as 12 top-five finishes. At season's end, Yarborough's 4,644 points placed him first in the championship standings (ahead of a fellow named Petty) and put an extra $453,404 in his pocket.

As successful as 1976 was for Yarborough and his Laguna, 1977 turned out to be even better. The season started off with a bang for the team at Daytona where, just one year after finishing last, Yarborough raced to his second Daytona 500 win. Cale added eight more wins to the victory column by the end of the 30-race series (along with 16 top-five finishes) to win his second consecutive Winston Cup championship.

On reflection, it appears that Yarborough's (and other drivers') Lagunas were a little too successful for their own good. At season's end the sanctioning body announced that use of the S-3 front fascia would be disallowed for 1978. As a result, Johnson, along with most other Laguna teams, shifted to Oldsmobile bodies for the new season.

One of the swoopy Lagunas that helped Cale Yarborough win two consecutive Winston Cup titles has been restored by Kim Haynes of Gastonia, North Carolina.

TECHNICAL INFORMATION

Wheelbase	115 inches
Weight	3,700 pounds
Front Suspension	Screw jack-adjustable, HD coils and fully fabricated control arms, twin shocks per wheel, sway bar
Rear Suspension	Screw jack-adjustable, HD coils, panhard rod, trailing arms, Ford 9-inch differential with floating hubs, twin shocks per wheel
Brakes	Ventilated discs
Engine	358-cubic-inch 1-4V, 550–650-horsepower V-8
Transmission	Borg Warner Super T-10, floor-shifted, four-speed manual
Speed at Darlington	153 miles per hour

The fans are fond of calling him "Awesome Bill from Dawsonville." But once upon a time Bill Elliott was simply George Elliott's red-haired son and not much known outside the foothills of north Georgia. Those days of anonymity came to an end, of course, with Elliott's domination of the NASCAR superspeedways during the mid-1980s and his capture of the fabled "Winston Million." But before Bill became the terror of the high banks, he spent years paying his dues as an also-ran on the circuit.

He began his quest for NASCAR superstardom accompanied by brothers Ernie and Dan in 1976. That was the year that Elliott first attempted to translate his north Georgia short-track-modified experience into success in the Winston Cup big leagues.

Race number one came at Rockingham in the Carolina 500, where Elliott started 34th and finished 33rd. All told, the not-yet-Awesome Bill made eight starts his first season

and failed to crack the top 10 at any one of them. Truth be known, his family- and Bill Champion-backed Fords were often the first to drop out of the races they entered in 1976, and Elliott won just $1,454 for his troubles.

The year 1977 wasn't much better for Bill, and of the 10 races he started, he finished better than 10th just twice. Things began to improve for Elliott the following season, when his dad bought several of the Cam 2-backed Mercurys that Bobby Allison had driven for Roger Penske in 1976. Though far from sleek, and consequently down in ultimate top speed, the new number 9 team cars were a significant improvement over the cars that Bill had driven before. That fact, coupled with Elliott's own improvements as a driver, quickly resulted in a greater number of top-10 finishes than Elliott had recorded before.

Like all Fords and Mercurys on the 1970s NASCAR scene, Elliott's red, black, and white Merc was powered by

Big as a house and sporting all manner of blunt perpendicular surfaces, the Mercurys that Bill Elliott campaigned during his first days on the NASCAR tour were anything but aerodynamic. Worse yet, the 351 Cleveland engines that powered them had to be cobbled up from junkyard sources, as Ford had been completely out of the racing game since the 1970 season. But brighter days were in the very near future for the not-yet "awesome Bill" and his lumbering Mercury.

When Bill Elliott first made his NASCAR debut, he drove "hand-me-down" Mercurys that his dad had purchased from Roger Penske's defunct Cam 2 racing operation. They were built over fabricated chassis that sported modified 1965 Galaxie and 9-inch Ford differential underpinnings.

a race-prepared version of the 351 Cleveland passenger car engine. Unlike today, where nearly every component of a Winston Cup Thunderbird's engine is available over the counter in re-engineered high-performance form, things were much bleaker for Fomoco racers in the 1970s. Ford's departure from factory-backed racing in 1969 had effectively turned off the tap as far as the development of new racing parts was concerned. As a result, by the late 1970s, die-hard Blue Oval types like the Elliotts were forced to race on junkyard parts and a few precious beefed-up blocks that had been purchased from Australia (where primitive road conditions resulted in beefier-than-state-side engine components). It was an undesirable situation for Ford racers and one big reason why the 1970s and early 1980s "belonged" to the Chevrolet *pilotos* on the circuit.

The 500-odd ponies cranked out by the Cleveland engine in Elliott's Mercury were used to power a "re-snouted" stock perimeter chassis. Fabricated front and rear frame sections mated to reinforced stock center chassis members formed the basis for the car's structure. Mild steel tubing was then added to the car's basic structure in the form of a NASCAR-spec roll cage.

The car's front suspension had been almost wholly lifted from the 1965 Galaxie line, while coil springs, Ford truck-evolved trailing arms, and a corporate differential made up the Merc's suspension. The cumbersome and wholly un-aerodynamic contours of the 1976 Mercury line were used to sheath the number 9 car's "Personals," and as mentioned, they, in turn, were coated in what was then Elliott's signature red, black, and white racing livery.

Race number one for Elliott and his new Mercury was the 1978 Daytona 500. Bill started sixth in the first of the twin qualifiers that year and finished fifth. That performance earned him a ninth-place berth on the starting grid of the 500 itself. When the green flag was given to the 41-car field, Elliott concentrated on staying out of trouble and running a consistent line. Though he failed to lead a lap that year, good luck, his new car's improved performance, and steady driving all conspired to produce an impressive eighth-place finish. Soon, Elliott was being

noticed by both the fans and other drivers on the tour. Four more top-10 finishes highlighted Elliott's 1978 season and helped earn him $42,065 in prize money.

Bill was back in his block-long Mercury in 1979. He started 13 Winston Cup races that year and again recorded a number of top-10 finishes. The first of those came at the spring Darlington race, where Elliott finished seventh in the Rebel 500. He backed that up with a convincing sixth in the Winston 500 at Talladega just one month later. Bill's best finish of the year came at Darlington in September, when he drove his renumbered (number 17) Mercury to a solid second-place finish in the Southern 500. Elliott started sixth that day, and by lap 118 he was in the lead of the oldest superspeedway event on the tour. At race's end he had been bested only by the Silver Fox, David Pearson.

Elliott spent one more season behind the wheel of his Mercury and made 11 more starts with its help. Four more top-10 finishes were in the record book by the end of that 31-race series. In that number was a seventh at Talladega in the Talladega 500, and a sixth at Charlotte in the National 500.

Elliott retired his Mercury prior to 1981, when a NASCAR rules change forced the entire field to downsize their racing chassis. Though he never visited victory lane in the car, Elliott's 1976 Mercury was still an important step toward the fame that was waiting for him just a few more seasons down the road.

South Florida's Donnie Gould today owns one of the Mercurys that Bill Elliott drove from 1978 to 1980.

TECHNICAL INFORMATION

Wheelbase	115 inches
Weight	3,700 pounds
Front Suspension	Screw jack-adjustable, HD coils and fully fabricated control arms, twin shocks per wheel, sway bar
Rear Suspension	Screw jack-adjustable, HD coils, panhard rod, trailing arms, Ford 9-inch differential with floating hubs, twin shocks per wheel
Brakes	Ventilated discs
Engine	358-cubic-inch 1-4V, 550–650-horsepower V-8
Transmission	Borg Warner Super T-10, floor-shifted, four-speed manual
Speed at Darlington	153 miles per hour

Marty Robbins was quite an interesting addition to the NASCAR scene. Though not a NASCAR driver by trade, he still quickly gained respect from the professional drivers who made every stop on the circuit. And though he only occasionally ventured out onto the track, Robbins often turned in a more-than-respectable performance when he did. Especially so since his favorite track was the always-intimidating 3.66-mile-long oval at Talladega.

So just who was this fellow Robbins, who wasn't a professional driver and who didn't race all that often? Well, he just happened to be one of the hottest stars in country and western music, and rather than racing for points or money, he showed up at NASCAR race tracks just for the sheer, unmitigated fun of it!

C&W fans of the 1950s and 1960s will recall the many hits that Robbins served up with regularity. One of his earliest chart toppers was entitled "A White Sport Coat and a Pink Carnation." He also found country music gold with tunes like "El Paso City" and "Devil Woman." His signature song involved a quick-on-the-draw cowboy and a fickle dance-hall girl named Rosa. It was simply called "El Paso," and today that song is still ranked as one of the greatest Western hits of all time.

Perhaps there was something of the gunfighter in Marty Robbins. Or maybe it was his Native American warrior ancestry that caused him to risk life and limb

Marty Robbins was one of country-western music's biggest stars before his untimely death. His Mopar stockers were a familiar—and popular—sight on the tour. One of Robbins' Magnums is currently on display at the International Motorsports Hall of Fame in Talladega, Alabama. Its yellow-and-purple paint scheme were anything but sedate. The car's performance was pretty hard to overlook, too. *Mike Slade*

on the Grand National superspeedways just for fun. Whatever his motivation, he was well received by his fellow drivers.

Marty's automotive brand of choice were cars of the Mopar persuasion. He had his own Dodge Daytona wing car built during the Aero Wars, and he qualified that car for the 1970 National 500 in Charlotte. Robbins' Daytona was painted a flashy combination of yellow and lavender and carried the number 42.

When NASCAR effectively outlawed all special-body aero-cars with a 5-liter engine limit in 1971, Robbins switched to Coke bottle-bodied Dodge Chargers. From 1973 to 1981, Robbins entered 19 Winston Cup events. The first of those outings (larks?) came in June of 1973 at College Station, Texas, in the Alamo 500. Robbins qualified his number 42 Charger 10th that day, and that placed the car ahead of many series regulars. Unfortunately, a traitorous 426 Hemi engine sidetracked Robbins' encouraging qualifying effort on lap 38. Robbins' next start, at Daytona in the Firecracker, ended much more acceptably with an eighth-place finish—ahead of such drivers as Darrell Waltrip, A.J. Foyt, Cale Yarborough, and Bobby Allison.

In due course, Robbins had the car updated to 1974 Charger trim, and in 1978 he had it rebodied as a Dodge Magnum. Along the way the car was involved in a number of racing shunts. The first occurred in the 1974 National 500 in Charlotte. The next came at Daytona in the 1975 500, and finally there was one at Talladega in the 1975 Winston 500. In each case he had the car shipped to Cotton Owens' Spartanburg, South Carolina, garage for repair. Robbins was quite partial to the car and was fond of telling all who would listen that it was the best car he had ever raced.

Unfortunately, Robbins was taken from both the racing and music worlds too soon. Though his songs still play daily on radio stations all across the country, Marty's Magnum today sits idle in the International Motorsports Hall

TECHNICAL INFORMATION

Wheelbase	110 inches
Weight	3,700 pounds
Front Suspension	Adjustable torsion bars, fully fabricated control arms, twin shocks per wheel
Rear Suspension	Screw jack-adjustable, HD leaf springs, Ford 9-inch differential with floating hubs, twin shocks per wheel
Brakes	Ventilated discs
Engine	358-cubic-inch 1-4V, 450–500-horsepower V-8
Transmission	Borg Warner Super T-10
Speed at Darlington	156 miles per hour

of Fame, trackside in Talladega, Alabama. Perhaps that's only fitting since nine of his last 19 outings took place at Talladega in either NASCAR or ARCA competition.

Like all Dodge stock cars of the era, Robbins' Magnum rolled on a reinforced unit-body chassis that had mounted torsion bars and fabricated control arms at the front and an 8 3/4-inch corporate differential at the rear. Disc brakes were employed to scrub off speed, and power was provided (in Magnum incarnation) by a race-spec Chrysler small-block engine.

Though Robbins never visited victory lane in any of his Dodge racing cars, it's certain that he had nearly as much fun just by taking the cars out on the track. It's a regrettable fact that the big business of NASCAR racing today makes having the same kind of fun that Robbins enjoyed an impossibility.

Though Richard Petty has earned the respect and love of Mopar partisans around the world, he has also broken their hearts on a number of occasions. During the early 1960s he drove a series of Belvedere-based race cars to scores of Grand National victories. In 1964, he turned the racing world upside down with the not-so-production but hellaciously fast 426 Hemi engine. In 1967, Petty earned the crown of "King of NASCAR" by winning 27 races (10 of them in a row!) in a boxy Petty Blue GTX.

But then, in 1969, Petty broke Plymouth fans' hearts for the first time by defecting to the Ford camp to secure a ride in the sleek Torino Talladegas that were the cars to beat that season. After that one-season dalliance, Petty was lured back to the true Mopar faith with the help of a winged Superbird and buckets of factory-sponsorship dollars. Once back in the fold, he

resumed his winning ways, and in 1971 he again dominated the circuit, winning 21 races on his way to yet another Grand National driving title.

In 1972 Petty switched allegiances to Dodge, but since that was still a car make in the Chryco family, it really wasn't thought of as a defection. For the next six seasons his Coke bottle-bodied Chargers were the class of any starting grid they graced. During that time Petty notched 37 Winston Cup wins and two more national driving titles.

The 1978 season brought with it a rules-mandated change to the cumbersome Dodge Magnum body style, and the brand-loyal Petty team tried to make a success of the new body style. Truth of the matter was, the Magnum was a butt-ugly car with all of the aerodynamic attributes of a brick. Yet Petty soldiered on with Dodge until the

Richard Petty broke the hearts of Mopar fans all across the country when he switched to Chevrolet in 1978. Though Petty had resisted that switch as long as he could, he was forced by racing realities to abandon his long-time affiliation with Dodge when the Magnum body style proved to be a loser. Petty's first GM race car was a Monte Carlo like this one. *Mike Slade*

1979 season. He even tried to make the new Mirada body style work, also. But when tests with a race-spec car proved it to be so slow that it couldn't coast back from the back stretch at Daytona when shut off at speed for a spark plug reading, Petty was forced to break his Mopar fans' hearts a second and final time. As Petty tells the story today, he loaded up the Mirada and carted it back to the garage in Randleman. By the end of the day, the car had been reskinned as a Monte Carlo.

And so it was that Richard Petty became a race car driver for the General Motors Corporation. As mentioned, Petty's first Chevrolet race car was a 1979 Monte Carlo, and one of those cars is pictured here. Though seemingly no better aerodynamically than the bulky Dodges that Petty had so recently abandoned, the car was actually slipperier than it appeared. It possessed another subtle yet significant advantage, too: big bulging fenders. And it was the Reubenesque proportions of those swoopy fenders that allowed more than a little race track contact without bending the bodywork down onto a tire.

The other advantage Petty found in his switch to the Bow Tie brigade was parts availability. By the end of the 1970s, the parts supply for Mopar racing engines had just about dried up. Famed Mopar crew chief Harry Hyde complained of having to race junkyard parts at about the same time that Petty made his switch to GM. Soon Hyde and all of the remaining Mopar racers made the same hard choice that Petty had to.

Petty's first race as a Chevrolet *piloto* took place at Michigan in the 1979 Champion Spark Plug 500. He qualified the car 14th for the race and wound up finishing in the same position due to a crash on lap 190. He was running in fifth place at the time and likely would have finished even higher in the standings had not a right front tire betrayed him. After the race, Petty good naturedly said, "We know how to build a Chevy, now we'll find out if we can fix one."

The car that Petty towed back to North Carolina for repair had begun life on the surface plate at Petty Enterprises in Randleman and was actually an eclectic mix of General Motors and Ford parts. Like most race cars of the day, the number 43 Monte Carlo actually rolled around on suspension components that had more in common with a 1965 Galaxie than anything that had ever been built on a Chevrolet assembly line. The same was true of the car's differential and transmission, too. The free-revving 358-cubic-inch small block bolted home between the front frame rails was, however, all Chevrolet. Screw jack-adjustable coil springs, 15x9-inch-wide rims, sticky Goodyear racing

TECHNICAL INFORMATION

Wheelbase	115 inches
Weight	3,700 pounds
Front Suspension	Screw jack-adjustable, HD coils and fully fabricated control arms, twin shocks per wheel, sway bar
Rear Suspension	Screw jack-adjustable, HD coils, panhard rod, trailing arms, Ford 9-inch differential with floating hubs, twin shocks per wheel
Brakes	Ventilated discs
Engine	358-cubic-inch 1-4V, 550–650-horsepower V-8
Transmission	Borg Warner Super T-10, floor-shifted, four-speed manual
Speed at Darlington	153 miles per hour

shoes, and a quartet of massive, vented disc brakes rounded out the car's suspension components.

Petty finished the 1979 season without a win, but things would significantly improve for him the following year. A harbinger of the good things ahead was the win that Petty scored in the 1979 Daytona 500. Petty's win was made all the more remarkable (it was his sixth triumph at that event, after all) by the fact that he had had 40 percent of his stomach surgically removed during the off-season and had been ordered to stay out of a race car for three months by his doctor. Petty scored that win in an Olds Cutlass, so that's another story.

Petty's first trip to victory lane in a Monte Carlo came at Martinsville in the Virginia 500 later that year. He scored other Bow Tie wins at Michigan in the Champion Spark Plug 500, at Dover in the CRC 500, and at Rockingham in the American 500, along with 20 other top-five finishes that season on his way to the Winston Cup national title. Petty won two more times in his Monte Carlo during the 1980 season before rules-mandated downsizing made those cars obsolete. One of Petty's STP Chevrolets is currently on display at his museum in Randleman, North Carolina.

There's no doubt about it, Dale Earnhardt will go down in the NASCAR record books as one of the greatest stock car drivers of all time. His 68 Winston Cup wins currently place him sixth on the all-time victory list (behind Richard Petty's 200 wins, David Pearson's 105 wins, Bobby Allison's 84 wins, Darrell Waltrip's 84 wins, and Cale Yarborough's 83 wins). Earnhardt's six Winston Cup national championships tie the six that King Richard Petty scored during his long and illustrious career.

Earnhardt's Winston Cup career began in 1975 with a back-of-the-pack finish in the World 600. Though Dale might have been disheartened by that performance (in which his Ed Negree-prepped Dodge was lapped 45 times by race winner Richard Petty), he didn't give up. By 1978 he had hooked up with the Rod Osterland Chevrolet team to score his first top-five finish in the Dixie 500 in Atlanta.

Earnhardt was back with Osterland for 1979 and in the hunt for rookie-of-the-year laurels. He drove a blue-and-yellow number 2 team Buick to an eighth-place finish at the Daytona 500 that year and then switched to a big-fendered Monte Carlo for short- and intermediate-track work. Earnhardt's first top-five for the team

that year came at North Wilkesboro in the Northwestern Bank 400. Dale's first career victory came at the very next race on the circuit, the Southeastern 500 at Bristol. His mount that day was a number 2 Monte Carlo identical to the one pictured here. By season's end, Earnhardt had added 10 more top-five finishes to that win to capture the hoped-for rookie honors and seventh place in the final points standings.

Though many rookie-of-the-year winners have faded from the racing scene shortly after capturing those honors, Earnhardt's 1980 sophomore season was a successful and record-breaking one. Dale began the season by signing a five-year pact with Rod Osterland. He began to give Osterland a return on his investment at the first race of the season at Riverside. Earnhardt qualified his big-fendered Monte Carlo fifth for the race at that multi-turn road course and then went on to finish second behind Darrell Waltrip's Monte Carlo. He switched mounts for the Daytona 500 in favor of a more-aerodynamic Olds Cutlass. During the race Earnhardt had the rounded nose of that number 2 car out in front on a number of occasions and ultimately came home in fourth.

More top-five finishes followed in quick order, and by the fifth event on the schedule, Earnhardt had

Dale Earnhardt was just a promising young driver and not NASCAR's feared "Intimidator" when he drove this yellow-and-blue Chevrolet Monte Carlo. But it didn't take long for the racing world to start paying attention to his daring on-track moves.

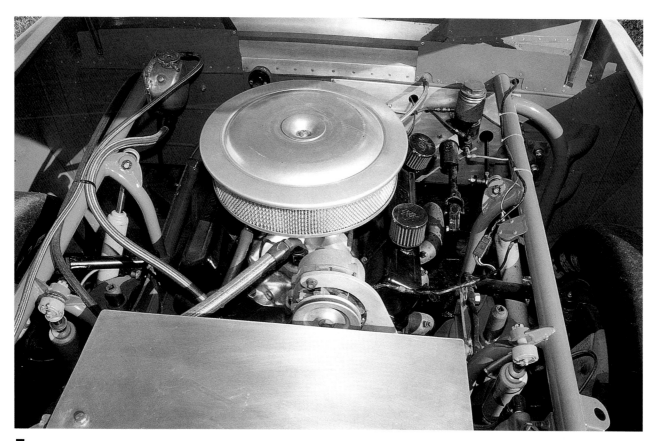

Though not as potent as the current "mouse" motors that carry Earnhardt into battle, the 358-cubic-inch iteration of the Chevrolet small-block engines that Earnhardt relied on in 1980 churned out nearly 600 horsepower in peak tune.

found the way to victory lane again. That win came in the Atlanta 500 in March. Though Dale had qualified his number 2 Chevrolet a disappointing 31st, he quickly found his way (or should that be forced his way?) to the front. He took the lead for good, ahead of rookie sensation Rusty Wallace, with 29 laps remaining to the line. After the race Earnhardt said, "This I could get used to. This beats the heck out of any other feeling I've had recently."

Just one race later in 1980, Earnhardt had his second chance to get used to the feeling of visiting victory lane, when he won the Southeastern 500 at Bristol. "I love it, I love it!" Earnhardt shouted as he climbed from his Chevrolet following the race. He went on to add, "When I joined Osterland, I really thought it would take a year to win my first race. But then we won this race last year, and we'll win our share this year. I don't see any reason why we can't win the Grand National championship this year."

Though a seemingly brash statement from a driver with only a relative handful of races under his belt, Earnhardt's statements after the race in Bristol proved to be a prediction of how the season would turn out. Earnhardt also visited victory lanes at Nashville, Martinsville, and Charlotte that season, and along the way, he recorded 14 other top-five finishes and earned

$671,990 in prize money. Oh, and by the way, he also won the 1980 Winston Cup national championship. That was the first time in NASCAR history that a Rookie-of-the-Year winner had come back the very next season to take top series honors.

When the NASCAR rules book mandated the use of downsized chassis for the 1981 season, Osterland and Earnhardt shifted to Pontiac-bodied race cars. Today one of the Monte Carlo race cars that Dale drove during his rookie year and first championship seasons is on display at the International Motorsports Hall of Fame in Talladega, Alabama. Like most late-1970s Winston Cup cars, Earnhardt's Chevrolet was built over a fully fabricated tubular steel frame that began life at Banjo Matthews' fabrication shop in Asheville, North Carolina. The chassis was turned into a roller with the installation of "front steer" Ford Galaxie-based front suspension components and an equally "Blue Oval" 9-inch differential. Long Chevy truck-evolved trailing arms and a cross-chassis panhard rod were used to keep the differential in check. Disc brakes and multi-piston calipers from the racing aftermarket were mounted all around, and they acted on a quartet of 15x9.5-inch steel rims shod in treadless bias ply Goodyear racing rubber.

Unlike modern-era Winston Cup cars, most of the sheet metal on the number 2 Monte Carlo was

Though bulbous and bulky appearing at first blush, the Monte Carlos that late-1970s Chevrolet racers like Dale Earnhardt fielded were actually very effective (if not aerodynamic) race cars. Their bulging fenders, for example, allowed more than a little "rubbing" without causing tire damage.

originally stamped out of sheet stock on a UAW line. Though some liberties were taken with wheel openings for tire clearance reasons, the Monte Carlo's body was basically stock.

As you might suspect, the cockpit of Earnhardt's car was a little short on comfort and convenience options. A single lightweight bucket seat served as the central focus, and it was augmented with additional bolt-on side bolsters. Once strapped in behind the foam-rimmed wheel, Earnhardt was confronted by a fabricated, sheet-metal dash that was filled with aftermarket gauges. The Hurst shifter he used to call up gears in the T-10 four-speed fell close at hand to Earnhardt's right. And so did the Chevrolet's on-board fire system. The whole package was encased in roll cage tubing that provided both protection and structural rigidity.

The Monte Carlo's bulging fenders were bludgeoned through the air with the aid of a full-race Chevrolet small-block engine. Based on the same design first introduced by Chevrolet in 1955, the willing little "mouse" motor featured a single four-barrel carburetor, and a single-plane "spider"-style intake manifold. Heavily massaged cast-iron heads carried oversized valves and an octet of roller rockers. Timing was provided for the forged steel and alloy reciprocating assembly by a cobby solid lifter camshaft. An external dry-sump oiling system and a pair of tubular headers completed the car's underhood appointments. In peak racing tune, the engine in Earnhardt's car could be relied on for something like 600 horsepower. And that was sufficient grunt to get the car around tracks like Charlotte and Atlanta at speeds in excess of 160 miles per hour.

TECHNICAL INFORMATION

Wheelbase	115 inches
Weight	3,700 pounds
Front Suspension	Screw jack-adjustable, HD coils and fully fabricated control arms, twin shocks per wheel, sway bar
Rear Suspension	Screw jack-adjustable, HD coils, panhard rod, trailing arms, Ford 9-inch differential with floating hubs, twin shocks per wheel
Brakes	Ventilated discs
Engine	358-cubic-inch 1-4V, 550–650-horsepower V-8
Transmission	Borg Warner Super T-10, floor-shifted, four-speed manual
Speed at Darlington	153 miles per hour

There wasn't much in the way of creature comforts in the cockpit of Earnhardt's Monte Carlo. A production-based bucket seat provided support. A foam-covered steering wheel and Hurst shifter fell close at hand, and when used in concert with the accelerator and brake pedal, they could be used to carve up a starting grid with surgical precision. As long as "Doctor" Earnhardt was at those controls, of course! The steering was not power-assisted.

When Darrell Waltrip first broke onto the NASCAR scene, it's fair to say that many in the garage area just didn't quite know how to take him. Though graced with natural good looks, great driving ability, and the tenacity and drive necessary to succeed in any endeavor, Waltrip was not exactly what you might call modest and self-effacing. No, quite the contrary, Waltrip was supremely confident to the point of arrogance.

As you might have guessed, Waltrip's outspoken nature didn't win him many friends in the garage area. In fact, during Waltrip's earliest days on the circuit, Cale Yarborough pinned the label "Jaws" on him. And it stuck. To be fair, part of D.W.'s problem was that he was one of the first of a new breed of drivers who had begun to challenge NASCAR's old guard. That alone could generate a fair amount of enmity for the brash young driver. Add to that Waltrip's highly skilled and aggressive driving style, and it's easy to understand why the racing establishment didn't greet him with open arms.

In 1972, Waltrip took his first laps around a NASCAR track, yet within two seasons, he was leading most every race he entered. In 1974, he came within a hair's breadth of winning the grand-daddy of all stock car races, the Southern 500 in Darlington, South Carolina. His second-place finish at the Lady in Black did nothing to diminish his self-confidence, and in 1975 Waltrip hired respected crew chief Jake Elder and began to predict imminent victory. And sure enough, win he did.

Win number one came at Waltrip's "home" track in Nashville, and shortly after taking the checkered flag, he signed his first big-time contract for a ride with the DiGard operation. Waltrip proved his first visit to victory lane would not be his last by quickly scoring his first win in a number 88 DiGard Chevrolet at Richmond in the Capital City 400.

By 1977, Waltrip was a regular visitor to the Winston Cup winner's circle. He notched his first super-speedway win that season (in the Rebel 400 at Darlington) and also posted five other short-track victories. Waltrip's winning ways continued into 1978, but even though he added six more Winston Cup trophies to his mantel, all was not sweetness and light inside the DiGard operation. D.W. had become convinced that he would be happier driving for another team, and said as much. Unfortunately, DiGard chief Bill Gardner felt otherwise, and he declined to release Waltrip from his multi-year contract. The tension between the two continued during the 1979 season even though Waltrip won six more times for the team (including triumphs at Darlington, Talladega, and Charlotte).

Waltrip finally gave Gardner 325,000 reasons to release him from his contract (and every one carried

When the NASCAR rules book mandated downsizing to a 110-inch wheelbase for the 1981 season, teams on the tour were in a quandary as to which cars to build. Junior Johnson opted for the Buick Regal, and that turned out to be a perfect choice. The Mountain Dew Buicks he built for Darrell Waltrip dominated the series for the next two seasons and won two of his three Winston Cup championships.

the likeness of George Washington) at the end of the 1980 season, after scoring five more victories for the DiGard team. Once free of his DiGard responsibilities, Waltrip quickly began negotiations with Junior Johnson. As it happened, Johnson was in search of a driver since long-time team *piloto* Cale Yarborough had just announced his departure after winning three back-to-back Winston Cup championships and scores of wins for the Rhonda, North Carolina-based operation.

Waltrip and Johnson came to terms quickly. After inking the contract, Waltrip commented that driving for Johnson was a "dream come true. When I was a little feller and started following races in the papers and on the radio, Junior was still driving. He was my hero."

When the new season dawned, it brought with it a new rule that downsized a Winston Cup car's chassis from 115 inches to 110 inches (the current standard).

Darrell Waltrip was one of the most successful drivers on the WC tour in the early 1980s. The races he won made good on the supreme confidence that he had displayed in his own abilities during the late 1970s. Though some in the garage area still called D.W. "Jaws," after the 1981 and 1982 seasons, they also had another name for him: The Champ.

Though seemingly a small change in dimension, the new rule actually required wholesale changes for every team on the circuit. Generally speaking, every team was forced to either build all-new cars from scratch or at least shorten all of their existing chassis. Rebodying the new or downsized platforms was a necessity. And since the aerodynamic performance of the resulting new cars was unknown, every team on the Winston Cup trail faced the 1981 season with more questions than answers about their cars' performance.

Waltrip's new comp cars were based on the Buick Regal. Built over a tubular steel frame, the cars rolled on front-steer underpinnings that had evolved from both the Ford Galaxie and Chevrolet truck lines. Screw jack-adjustable coil springs, a wrist-thick front sway bar and cross-chassis panhard rod, and manhole-sized, ventilated disc brakes all played a part in that chassis' construction.

Waltrip's 1981 mounts came clothed in a mostly hand-formed sheet-metal skin that closely resembled the bodywork found on a showroom Regal. Though not an optimal body for high-banks work due to its formal roof and nearly vertical back light, Waltrip's Regal did possess the advantage of a low hood line that terminated in an angled grille. When dressed in the flashy Mountain Dew racing livery that reflected the team's 1981 sponsorship, the car was one of the best-looking on the racing grid.

It was also one of the fastest. Waltrip drove that point home at Richmond where, in only his second outing for the team, he put the number 11 small-block Chevrolet-powered Buick in victory lane at the Richmond 400. Win number two followed quickly, and Waltrip beat Dale Earnhardt to the checker at Rockingham in the Carolina 500. Win number three came at Bristol in the Valleydale 500, and the team's first super-

speedway triumph was recorded at the World 600 in Charlotte. All told, Waltrip and the Dew Crew visited victory lane a total of 12 times in that first season together. Those wins, coupled with 21 top-five finishes, earned Waltrip $799,134 and his first Winston Cup national driving title.

Waltrip almost duplicated that performance the following season, when he once again drove the Dew Buick to 12 more Winston Cup wins. That 1982 "victory tour" made stops at the winner's circle in Talladega (twice), Atlanta, North Wilkesboro (twice), Bristol, Dover, Martinsville, and Rockingham. Those 12 wins and 17 top-five finishes earned Waltrip his second-consecutive Winston Cup championship. It was an incredible performance.

Waltrip's Mountain Dew Buicks were rebodied into Chevrolet Monte Carlo SSes for 1983 as the second version of the factory Aero Wars got under way. He and Johnson stayed together through the 1986 season and scored many more victories (not to mention Waltrip's third Winston Cup title in 1985).

Though some of the Winston Cup Buicks that Waltrip drove in 1981 and 1982 have survived in other incarnations, none of them exist today in Mountain Dew Regal trim.

TECHNICAL INFORMATION

Wheelbase	110 inches
Weight	3,700 pounds
Front Suspension	Screw jack-adjustable HD coils, fully fabricated control arms, twin shocks per wheel, sway bar
Rear Suspension	Screw jack-adjustable HD coils, panhard rod, trailing arms, Ford 9-inch differential with floating hubs, twin shocks per wheel
Brakes	Ventilated discs
Engine	358-cubic-inch 1-4V, 450–500-horsepower V-8
Transmission	Borg Warner Super T-10, floor-shifted, four-speed manual
Speed at Darlington	155 miles per hour

RUSTY WALLACE'S 1986-1987 PONTIAC 2+2

Rusty Wallace has proven to be one of the most popular and successful drivers on the NASCAR Winston Cup tour. As of 1995, Wallace had notched an impressive 41 wins, and he ranked 12th on the all-time victory list. In 1989, Wallace bested the entire NASCAR field to win his first Winston Cup national driving title. And, since his driving days are far from over, there's every possibility that he'll be adding both wins and national championships to that tally.

But back in 1980, Wallace was just another aspiring stock car driver hoping to find a way to park his race car in the NASCAR garage area. Though the then bushy-haired 24-year-old Missouri native had been quite successful in the USAC car ranks (and, in fact, was that cir-

Pontiac was one of the combatants in the second factory Aero Wars. The 1986 Aero Coupes that drivers like Rusty Wallace and Richard Petty drove in that "conflict" were every bit as swoopy as the Talladegas and Daytonas that had battled it out during the first factory-backed Aero Wars. Like those earlier competition cars, Pontiac's Aero Coupes had been designed with minimum aerodynamic drag in mind.

Rusty Wallace was the only driver to make the Pontiac Aero Coupe work. The victories he scored with his number 27 Blue Max team cars turned out to be the only ones scored by any long-nosed/bubble-back Pontiac driver. Interestingly, those wins all came on short tracks and not on the superspeedways the cars had been designed to dominate.

cuit's rookie of the year), his closest view of a NASCAR finish line had been from a grandstand seat. But that all changed in early 1980 when he got a call from a fellow named Penske about a race car deal. The Penske in question was *the* Roger Penske, famed driver in his own right and winning Indy car team owner. Penske had dabbled in the NASCAR ranks from time to time, too, and during the 1970s he had even fielded a team of red, white, and blue Winston Cup stock cars for both Mark Donohue and Bobby Allison.

As it turns out, Penske was thinking about making a return to the NASCAR ranks on a limited basis for the 1980 season, and Wallace's performance on the USAC trail had caught his eye. Phone calls were made and agreements reached. The new combination made its debut at Atlanta in March of 1980. Their pairing was an instant success. Wallace's unfamiliarity with the high-banked oval at Atlanta was in no way apparent during qualifying, and when initial heats were over he reserved a spot for his blue-and-white number 16 Impala on the fourth row of the starting grid. At race's end he was second only to another fresh face on the circuit, a fellow named Earnhardt. After the race Wallace said, "I never

thought we could take a brand new car and a brand new driver and do that well."

By the time the 1986 season rolled around, Wallace had become a series regular and was team driver for Raymond Beadle's Blue Max operation. Rusty's competitive mounts that year were swoopy Pontiac Aero Coupes designed by General Motors to counter the aerodynamic advantage that Ford Thunderbirds had enjoyed since 1983. Based on the factory LeMans body style, an Aero Coupe sported a radically extended and lowered snout that was designed to more efficiently cut through the air. A special add-on "bubble-back" rear window was grafted onto the car's bustle to complete the aero upgrade.

Pre-season shakedown runs with the new car were promising, and Wallace started the season with high hopes of scoring his first Winston Cup win. He didn't have to wait long. Wallace got the season off to a good start with an eighth-place finish in the Daytona 500, and he scored another top-10 finish in the Miller High Life 400 at Richmond just two weeks later.

Wallace notched yet another eighth-place finish in the Motorcraft 500 at Atlanta before rolling into Bristol for the Valleydale 500 in April. Though Rusty could only muster a 14th-place starting berth for his long-

Though the Pontiac crest might have adorned the flanks of Wallace's Aero Coupe, a Chevrolet small-block engine was just a sheet-metal thickness away. Like all GM-based Winston Cup cars since 1978, Wallace's car relied on Bow Tie power for motorvation.

nosed Pontiac, by midpoint of the 500-lap event, he put the number 27 car in the lead. After dicing with Bobby Allison, Darrell Waltrip, and Dale Earnhardt for supremacy, Wallace took the lead for the final time on lap 399. The next 101 laps saw Wallace stretch out a commanding 10-second lead over the next-closest rival, Ricky Rudd, and Rusty maintained that margin right up to the checker. It was the first win for Wallace, the first win for his new crew chief Barry Dodson, and the first victory scored by a "bubble-back" Pontiac. It would not be the last.

After the race, a jubilant Dodson said, "A lot of people have doubted this team because we haven't won in a while. Some people doubted Rusty's ability. But anyone who has won 200 short-track races is a winner. Some people doubted he would ever make it big. Well, he made it big today. Mark this date." Mark that date indeed.

Wallace scored his second career victory in September of that year at the Goody's 500 in Martinsville. He went on to round out the season with 14 other top-10 finishes on his way to a sixth-place finish in the seasonal points chase.

Wallace re-upped with the Blue Max team in 1987 and once again found himself at the wheel of a swoopy Pontiac Aero Coupe. Win number three came on the road course at Watkins Glen, where Rusty's Kodiak-sponsored Poncho led second-place finisher Terry Labonte across the stripe. Rusty made 1987 a "road course" year by winning the Winston Western 500 at Riverside just before the season came to a close in November. Fourteen other top-10 finishes helped Wallace improve his position to fifth in the overall points standings for 1987.

Rusty retired his long-nosed Pontiacs in favor of the new Grand Prix body style for 1988, and so ended the brief career of Pontiac's special aero variant. Though designed for superspeedway supremacy, the long-nosed Aero Coupe was destined never to score a high-speed win. In fact, of all the drivers to campaign the Aero Coupe, Wallace was the only NASCAR driver to drive one of the cars into victory lane.

One of Rusty's Aero Coupes has been returned to the track in vintage trim by Phil Bradbury of Lexington, Kentucky.

The fuel cell in Wallace's Aero Coupe was limited to a NASCAR-spec 22-gallon maximum. A steel can was used to hold that foam-filled bladder in place and protect it from punctures. Note the stubby nature of the trunk opening created by the Aero Coupe's extended rear window.

TECHNICAL INFORMATION

Wheelbase	110 inches
Weight	3,700 pounds
Front Suspension	Screw jack-adjustable HD coils, fully fabricated control arms, single gas shock per wheel, sway bar
Rear Suspension	Screw jack-adjustable, HD coils, panhard rod, trailing arms, Ford 9-inch differential with floating hubs, single gas shock per wheel
Brakes	Ventilated discs
Engine	358-cubic-inch 1-4V, 600–650-horsepower V-8
Transmission	Borg Warner Super T-10, floor-shifted, four-speed manual
Speed at Darlington	158 miles per hour

Ford's departure from racing in the early 1970s effectively made NASCAR a General Motors playground. Though die-hard Fomoco teams like the Wood Brothers and Bud Moore soldiered on with the leftover parts still in their inventory, GM-powered cars essentially had a lock on both victory lane and the NASCAR championship. Until 1983, that is. For that was the year that Ford's all-new, radically (for the time) rounded-off Thunderbirds first began showing up on Winston Cup starting grids. Their slick aerodynamic profile, coupled with increased factory interest (read: funding) in racing, quickly made certain red-haired fellows from Georgia, and their number 9 Ford race cars, household names.

Suddenly, GM's boxy, vertical-rear-windowed intermediates were no longer the fastest cars on the track. Ford victories began to multiply alarmingly. In 1985, Thunderbird drivers equaled their GM counterparts in the total number of wins. The 14 victories they achieved that season were the most scored by Ford since 1969. Something had to be done to stem the "Blue Oval" tide, and both Pontiac and Chevrolet aerodynamic engineers began to work on the problem.

One of the cars that resulted from that off-season activity was the Pontiac 2+2. Based on the Grand Prix intermediates that had been in service since 1981, the new Aero Warriors featured an assortment of new body panels that had all been designed specifically for use on NASCAR superspeedways. Round two of the factory-backed Aero Wars first waged in 1969 had begun.

Just like the Talladegas, Spoiler IIs, Charger Daytonas, and Superbirds that had first vied for aerodynamic supremacy nearly two decades before, the new, special-bodied Pontiacs were designed with low coefficient-of-drag numbers in mind. At the bow, an all-new drooped and extended nose cone had been grafted on to help slice through the wall of air that was encountered at racing speeds. The most notable change made to the

When Richard Petty jumped to GM in 1978, the first cars he campaigned for the "General" were Chevrolets. He switched sheet metal allegiance to Pontiac in 1982 and finished out his career as a "Poncho" pilot. He drove swoopy bubble-back Aero Coupes in 1986 and 1987.

A big part of the Aero Coupe package was the special droop snout the cars carried. Like the Talladega design that Ralph Moody penned in 1969, that special nose was designed to slip through the air like a hot knife through butter.

Pontiac engineers grafted on a bubble-back rear window to round out the Aero Coupe package. It worked to smooth out airflow over the roof and hindquarters of the car.

standard Grand Prix unit body was the addition of a huge bubbled back light that was designed to reduce the destabilizing lift created by a stock GM intermediate's vertical rear window. The end result was a roof line that flowed in a nearly unbroken arc from the A-pillars to the deck-lid-mounted rear spoiler. The total package was not too dissimilar in silhouette from the Ford aero-variants that dominated the high banks in 1969.

When the field for the 1986 Daytona 500 rolled out to take the green flag, Richard Petty and seven other 2+2 drivers were among the race's 42 starters. Unfortunately, though the new Poncho's swoopy bodywork looked fast both on paper and in the flesh, once at speed the car proved to be a tick off the pace. Petty's 2+2 retired early after an unplanned close encounter with the turn-three wall. Other bubble-back-Pontiac drivers fared somewhat better, and three finished the race in the top 10. That was pretty much the story for 2+2 drivers in both 1986 and 1987: close but no cigar.

Though Petty didn't win with his Aero Coupe, he never lost his trademark smile. His impressive—and unmatchable—career encompassed 200 Grand National/Winston Cup victories and six National Driving Championships. Incredible.

All told, aero-variant Pontiacs took part in 58 Winston Cup events, winning four and recording top-five finishes in 24 others. Rusty Wallace accounted for all of Pontiac's wins those two seasons. It's truly ironic to note that though his Kodiak-backed Pontiac 2+2s had been designed with high-speed aerodynamics in mind, Wallace's wins came at Bristol, Martinsville, Watkins Glen, and Riverside—all tracks where superspeedway streamlining is not of paramount importance.

In 1988, Pontiac introduced a new, more rounded-off Grand Prix body style that Wallace ultimately drove to his first Winston Cup driving championship.

TECHNICAL INFORMATION

Wheelbase	110 inches
Weight	3,700 pounds
Front Suspension	Screw jack-adjustable, HD coils, fully fabricated control arms, single gas shock per wheel, sway bar
Rear Suspension	Screw jack-adjustable HD coils, panhard rod, trailing arms, Ford 9-inch differential with floating hubs, single gas shock per wheel
Brakes	Ventilated discs
Engine	358-cubic-inch 1-4V, 600–650-horsepower V-8
Transmission	Borg Warner Super T-10, floor-shifted, four-speed manual
Speed at Darlington	158 miles per hour

Though Darrell Waltrip had won scores of races and no fewer than three Winston Cup championships in his career by the end of the 1986 season, there was still one "big one" that had gotten away. And that elusive, never-captured prize was the Daytona 500. Though many successful drivers spend a whole career on the NASCAR circuit and never visit victory lane even one time, Waltrip, by 1986, had just about memorized the winner's circle at every track across the country. Save for Daytona, that is. And, like Dale Earnhardt today (who also has yet to taste victory in the 500), it really galled D.W. to the point that he rated Daytona as his least-favorite track. And when you consider the major wreck he had in the 1983 500 in concert with his total lack of success at the "Big D," it's pretty easy to understand Waltrip's dislike for the track.

But that all changed in 1989. The car that finally helped D.W. find the way to victory lane at Daytona was a long-nosed, bubble-back version of the Chevrolet Monte Carlo. Built with a special nose-extending front

fascia and "add-on" air-smoothing fastback rear window, the Chevy was GM's answer to the aerodynamically superior Thunderbirds that Ford racers had debuted in 1983.

At that particular time, "boxy" was in on the NASCAR circuit. The Monte Carlos that Chevy drivers "rode" into battle at the time featured formal roof lines with nearly vertical back lights and equally upright grille areas that caught the wind as effectively as an open parachute. That drag, coupled with the lift created by the car's formal roof line, was tolerable only so long as the competition was as equally afflicted with its own aerodynamic woes. And that had been just the case in the Ford camp until 1983. Few cars were as squared-off and boxy as the Ford Thunderbird had been prior to the model change year of 1983. The new 'Birds that had been unveiled that year were a different story. Based on an entirely fresh sheet of styling studio paper, Ford's new personal luxury cars were rounded everywhere and swoopy to the max. Chevrolet racers

Darrell Waltrip hated going to Daytona for nearly two decades. And that's because he just never had any luck there, especially at the all-important Daytona 500. All of that changed in 1989 when he finally won the "Big One" with a number 17 Tide Monte Carlo.

D.W.'s Monte Carlo was powered by a Hendrick team-prepared small-block Chevrolet engine. It was housed beneath a tube-reinforced hood skin and within the confines of a fabricated chassis snout and roll cage "loop." Note the aluminum ducting around the alloy radiator.

never saw the T-Bird truck that hit them and quickly began to search about for an improved version of the Monte Carlo to counter the new aero threat.

The first step in that process involved stealing a bit of the aerodynamic wizardry that Ralph Moody had employed to make his Torino Talladegas the winners of the factory-backed Aero Wars in 1969 and 1970. Like Moody before them, Chevy engineers cooked up an extended nose cone for the Monte Carlo body that both lowered and tapered the car's front profile. Trouble was, that new nose didn't completely solve the problem as the cars' squared-off rear window still created gobs of unwanted lift at superspeedway velocities (as Cale Yarborough's wild qualifying ride at the 1983 Daytona 500 had proven in spades). Chevrolet stylists finally solved that problem in 1986 by grafting on a special bubble-back rear window that essentially completed the Bow Tie replication of the original fastback Torino Talladega silhouette. GM homologated the new Aero Warrior in time for the 1986 season. And the new design turned out to be one of the most successful "Chevrolet" racing designs of all time.

As mentioned, it was just one such Monte Carlo SS that opened the door to Daytona's victory lane in 1989. The particular car in question was a brightly hued "Tide

Team" SS that had been prepared for Waltrip by the Hendrick racing operation. As long-time NASCAR fans will recall, Waltrip went to the Hendrick team upon his departure from the Junior Johnson operation in 1987. Although the Hendrick operation was well-funded and boasted one of the newest racing shops on the circuit (located just down the road from the Charlotte Motor Speedway), Waltrip had not been able to find the same level of immediate success with Hendrick that he had enjoyed as a Junior Johnson driver. In fact, he visited victory lane just one time (at Martinsville) during his first year with the team. Only two Winston Cup victories had been forthcoming during the following year (at the World 600 and at Pannil Sweatshirts 500 at Martinsville).

When the 1989 season dawned, Waltrip was hoping for better luck for the Tide Team. And that's just what he got. Waltrip got off to a good start during speed weeks 1989, with a qualifying run just a few ticks of the stop watch slower than pole-sitter (and Hendrick teammate) Ken Schrader's 196.966-mile-per-hour hot lap. Waltrip's performance earned him an unobstructed view of the track from the outside pole starting position when the green flag was unfurled.

Once the race was under way, D.W. leaped ahead of Schrader and led the first 10 laps in a race that, at first,

One of the secrets behind Waltrip's Daytona 500 win was his Chevrolet's aerodynamic package. Taking a page from the same book that Ralph Moody had used to create the Torino Talladega in 1969, Chevrolet engineers used a stretched snout and a fastback rear window to smooth out airflow over the car at speed. Just as in 1969, it worked!

seemed destined to be determined by top speed. Waltrip went on to claim the lead on three other occasions during the race for a total of 25 laps. But it wasn't Waltrip's speed so much as it was his savvy that ultimately carried the day for the number 17 Tide Team car. As Waltrip recounted later, "We started thinking about lap 165 that it might go green the rest of the way. I asked Jeff (crew chief Jeff Hammond) if we could make it. He and the crew did some figuring and came back on the radio and told me that if we did, it would be close." And indeed it was. So close that Waltrip ran out of gas as he pulled into victory lane. But it was, after all, after he had already won the race! Waltrip was so exuberant about his victory that he broke into dance in victory lane. After trying to unlock that particular door for 17 long years, he had finally parked his number 17 car in Daytona's victory lane.

The Tide Monte Carlo that D.W. drove to victory that day is currently on display at Hendrick's Motorsports Museum, located just outside of the team's shop in Harrisburg, South Carolina.

Specially fabricated aluminum bucket seats had replaced their production-based predecessors by the mid-1980s. They offered infinitely more support—and safety—than the seats that drivers had relied on in previous seasons. Note the fabricated dash, special racing steering wheel, and on-board fire extinguishing system that was also part of the Tide car's cockpit.

In addition to being faster than stink and as slippery as a politician in an election year, D.W.'s Monte Carlo was one of the best-looking cars on the NASCAR tour. It looked especially fetching when parked in victory lane!

TECHNICAL INFORMATION

Wheelbase	110 inches
Weight	3,700 pounds
Front Suspension	Screw jack-adjustable HD coils, fully fabricated control arms, single gas shock per wheel, sway bar
Rear Suspension	Screw jack-adjustable, HD coils, panhard rod, trailing arms, Ford 9-inch differential with floating hubs, single gas shock per wheel
Brakes	Ventilated discs
Engine	358-cubic-inch 1-4V, 600–650-horsepower V-8
Transmission	Borg Warner Super T-10, floor-shifted, four-speed manual
Speed at Darlington	158 miles per hour

Back in the 1960s, Joni Mitchell used to sing about not knowing what you've got 'til it's gone. And was she ever right! Take for example the super slippery 1987–1988 Thunderbirds that, for the time, were the fastest cars to ever circle a NASCAR track. Few would have guessed then that the cars were arguably the best NASCAR stock car ever built. It's equally certain that more than a few Ford NASCAR teams would give a number of their body parts to be able to field such cars again. But like the lady said, you don't know what you've got 'till it's gone!

Things were more than a little bleak for the Ford faithful for most of the 1970s (and early 1980s). Lee Iacocca's decision to get Ford out of factory-backed racing in 1969 pretty much slammed the door on the Total Performance era. Holman & Moody closed up shop shortly after the withdrawal of factory support, and soon races that Ford drivers had "owned" for nearly a decade were being won by Brand X cars. Even worse, some of those Brand X cars carried Bow Ties on their engine blocks, and Chevy hadn't won a NASCAR race since its own retreat from motorsports in 1963.

Things had only gotten worse for Ford racers as the 1970s unfolded and soon, not only were high-perfor-

mance parts in short supply (Iacocca's decision had terminated race engine development and production, too), worse yet, the cars they were forced to race were as boxy and aerodynamic as a load of concrete blocks. The nadir was reached in 1981 and 1982, when the Ford Thunderbird line featured more sharp edges than a brick. Something had to be done—and soon—or the few remaining Ford race teams, like those of Bud Moore and the Wood Brothers, would likely jump ship and make NASCAR an all-General Motors series.

Fortunately, Ford's anti-race pendulum had swung its farthest by 1982 and finally had begun to inch back toward racing sponsorship. With Iacocca now cranking out Chrysler K cars, some inside the Dearborn Glass house began to remember the sales benefits of factory-backed motorsports. Soon the order was put in for R&D work on high-performance parts, and even a "Special Vehicles" racing division was set up.

Ford racers got the best news yet in 1983, when an all-new Thunderbird body style was unveiled. Gone were the sharp edges and air-catching vertical surfaces of the year before. In their place, stylists had penned flowing curves and rounded edges that were

Bud Moore is one of the most stalwart of the Fomoco faithful. He has fielded Fords and Mercurys since 1964. His Thunderbirds carried Motorcraft racing livery in 1987 and were campaigned by Ricky Rudd.

Though not readily apparent at first, Thunderbirds like those driven by Ricky Rudd in 1987 and 1988 turned out to be the fastest NASCAR competition cars of all time. The NASCAR rules book will likely keep things that way, since the triple-digit speeds turned in by those cars in 1987 scared the sanctioning body into reinstating the restrictor plate rule in 1988.

guaranteed to slip more readily through the air than the Thunderbirds that had gone before. Who can forget the incredible domination a fellow named Elliott enjoyed on the superspeedways during the early 1980s? Aerodynamics and a renewed supply of Ford-developed high-performance parts were key to that success.

Just when it seemed that things couldn't get any better for Ford racers on the circuit, Ford stylists rolled out an all-new Fox-chassised Thunderbird design for the 1987 model year. At first blush, it looked as if the car had been designed at a NASCAR track and not in a Motown studio. And you know, perhaps it had been.

Take, for example, the new 'Bird's nose piece. Kicked out toward a bumper that had been relocated forward, it nearly begged for the inevitable NASCAR-spec "snow plow" front spoiler to complete the sweeping line created by the plunging hood. In the rear, the bustle had been raised a significant number of inches, and that new, higher body line was guaranteed to make a NASCAR-spec rear spoiler work more effectively. When these new features were welded and pop-riveted

in place over a Winston Cup chassis and dressed out in hand-formed side bodywork, the resulting competition car was arguably the most aerodynamic NASCAR warrior ever built.

And that's just what qualifying speeds at Daytona and Talladega soon revealed. Hot lap speeds at Daytona in 1987 jumped a full 5 *miles an hour*. Where Bill Elliott had turned in a pole speed of 205.039 with his 1986 Thunderbird, the same car and essentially the same engine were able to up that velocity to 210.036 with just the addition of 1987 Thunderbird sheet metal the following year. Similar improvements in speed were also noted at Talladega. Bill Elliott's Winston 500 qualifying speed for the 1987 running of that event was a blistering 212.809 miles per hour.

Few knew it at the time, but that lap will probably remain the fastest stock car lap of all time. The reason? The dreaded, horsepower-robbing restrictor plate that the sanctioning doges put back in service at the close of the 1987 season. In the blink of an eye, speeds fell nearly 10 miles per hour at both tracks, and racing at Daytona and Talladega became follow-the-leader

Rudd's Motorcraft car was powered by a racing evolution of the familiar small-block Cleveland engine. The canted-valve cylinder heads common to the Cleveland family flowed air the way Niagara Falls flows water. Cubic feet per minute translate into buckets of horsepower in the mechanical realm. When coupled with superior aerodynamics, those ponies made 220-mile-per-hour backstretch speeds just a tickle of the throttle away.

freight-train affairs where passing is uncommon and multi-car wrecks are the norm. Those same conditions prevail today.

Bud Moore of Spartanburg, South Carolina, was one of the team owners who had the good fortune to field a 1987–1988 Thunderbird-based team. Moore's team was (and still is) one of the oldest in the Ford stable. Moore's tenure with Fomoco dates back to 1963, when he switched from Pontiacs to a fleet of

red, black, and white number 8 Mercury Marauders. Little Joe Weatherly was Moore's driver that season, and he used his Merc's performance to secure his second-straight Grand National driving championship. Over the years, Moore also provided Ford and Mercury rides for drivers like Billy Wade, Darel Dieringer, Tiny Lund, Darrell Waltrip, Bobby Isaac, Bobby Allison, and Buddy Baker.

The driver of the number 15 Motorcraft car for 1987 was soft-spoken Virginia driver Ricky Rudd. Rudd kicked off the team's season with a ninth-place finish in the Daytona 500. Victory number one for the team came at Atlanta, where Rudd qualified sixth and translated that starting berth into victory. It was Rudd's second career superspeedway victory. Rudd scored a second Motorcraft team win in 1987 at Dover in the Delaware 500, where he outpaced Davey Allison's number 29 Thunderbird to the checkered flag. In addition to those triumphs, Rudd also scored eight other top-five finishes on his way to a sixth-place finish in the season's point standings.

Rudd scored one more win for the team the next season on the road course at Watkins Glen in August of 1988. Other top-five finishes, including seconds at Richmond, North Wilkesboro, and Rockingham helped Rudd finish 11th in the 1988 points race.

A new Thunderbird body style was introduced in 1989. Though at first blush the new car appeared to be an improvement on the old design, it wasn't, and as a result, Ford drivers haven't enjoyed the same level of success since. Interestingly, a faithful

Rudd's Motorcraft car was strikingly good-looking. It was more than just a pretty face, however, and the diminutive Virginia native drove the car to two wins and 10 top-10 finishes in 1987.

Like all NASCAR cars of the modern era, Rudd's number 15 car sported a cocoon-like structure of roll cage tubing that both stiffened its handling resolve and provided for driver safety. Note the quick-release steering wheel and on-board fire system that also helped make Rudd's "office" an OSHA-friendly workplace.

reproduction of the 1987–1988 Thunderbird has recently been put to work on the high banks. That particular car possesses the same sloping hood line and forward-mounted bumper that characterized the old T-Bird body style. The new car in question also features a raised and widened bustle, much like the hind feathers found on a 1987–1988 'Bird. What car is it, you ask, that captures all of the superior aerodynamic qualities embodied in the 1987–1988 Thunderbird line? The new 1995–1996 Monte Carlo, of course.

One of the Ford Thunderbirds that Ricky Rudd drove for Bud Moore has recently returned to the track in vintage action. It belongs to Dale Nichols of Orlando, Florida.

TECHNICAL INFORMATION

Wheelbase	110 inches
Weight	3,700 pounds
Front Suspension	Screw jack-adjustable, HD coils, fully fabricated control arms, single gas shock per wheel, sway bar
Rear Suspension	Screw jack-adjustable, HD coils, panhard rod, trailing arms, Ford 9-inch differential with floating hubs, single gas shock per wheel
Brakes	Ventilated discs
Engine	358-cubic-inch 1-4V, 650–675-horsepower (unrestricted) V-8
Transmission	Borg Warner Super T-10, floor-shifted, four-speed manual
Speed at Darlington	158 miles per hour

Davey Allison was born the son of a race car driver and the nephew of yet another racer. So perhaps it was inevitable that he would grow up to be one himself. But not quite as soon as he would have liked. It seems that young Davey caught the racing bug early, and so thoroughly was he under the spell of Winston Cup racing that his grades in school began to suffer. According to teachers in the schools he attended, young Davey had racing on the brain just about 24 hours a day.

Before long, Davey was hounding his dad, Bobby, for a chance to race a car of his own—just like his dad did. Wisely, Bobby turned away all such requests until Davey had finished school. And even then, he didn't allow the lad to go racing until he had paid his dues by working around his father's race shop in Hueytown, Alabama. Though Davey, like his dad, had been born in Miami, Florida, he had grown up in Alabama as the youngest member of racing's "Alabama Gang." And when he first got permission to go racing, he followed the footsteps first laid down by his dad and uncle Donnie at south Florida's Opa Locka Speedway by first trying his hand at modified racing.

Those first forays into racing were in 1979. By 1985, young Davey was ready for bigger things. His first taste of the Winston Cup big league came at his "hometown" superspeedway in Talladega. He drove a Chevrolet for veteran car owner Hoss Ellington that day, and Davey's promise as a driver was crystal clear by the end of the race. Though it was his first time in competition on the fastest of all the superspeedways, Davey brought his race car home in 10th. Davey made two more starts for Ellington that season.

He hooked up with the Sadler racing team for 1986 and made appearances at five Winston Cup events. In 1987, he put his career in high gear by making a run for Rookie-of-the-Year honors (a title his uncle Donnie had won in 1967).

Davey's team for his first full year on the circuit was the same one that had previously fielded cars for his father, Bobby. Owned by Harry Ranier, the team relied on Thunderbirds for motorvation, and the engines in those cars were prepared by a fellow named Robert Yates. Yates was the same mechanic who, while working at Holman & Moody, built the 427 Tunnel Port engine that had powered LeeRoy

Davey Allison burst onto the NASCAR scene like a comet burning bright with potential. The Robert Yates-prepped Thunderbirds he drove played a large role in young Davey's dazzling debut. He became one of the fastest men in NASCAR history in 1987 when he drove a swoopy Havoline T-Bird like this one around Daytona at 198.05 miles per hour in July of that year.

Maximum warp speeds were made possible by the slippery shape of Allison's Thunderbird. The snow-plow-like beak kicked air up and over the hood, and the rounded roof then gently channeled it back to the raised bustle and downforce-generating rear-deck spoiler. After only two years of superspeedway duty, the 1987 and 1988 T-Bird body style was retired in favor of a new design that's proven to be less aerodynamic.

Yarbrough's Torino Talladega to victory in the 1969 Daytona 500. Yates had also built the engines that had made Bobby Allison's long-sought 1983 Winston Cup Championship a reality. So hooking up with the Ranier operation was in many ways a homecoming for the young man.

First up for Davey in 1985 was qualifying for the Daytona 500 in February of that year. When the dust settled, Davey had put his number 28 Havoline T-Bird on the outside pole. It was only the second time in NASCAR history that a rookie had put his car on the front row at the "Super Bowl of stock car racing." Bad luck in the race itself resulted in a disappointing 27th-place finish, but he found the way to victory lane just three months later. The setting for that first Winston Cup win was a fitting one, since it came at Talladega.

Davey qualified third for the Winston 500 that year and then led much of the way to win a race that had boasted the fastest starting field in racing history (Bill Elliott sat on the pole with a qualifying speed of 212.809 miles per hour). Davey won a second time that year at Dover and easily cinched Rookie-of-the-Year honors.

Though it probably wasn't much appreciated at the time, the 1987 Thunderbirds that Davey (and others) campaigned that season were the fastest racing cars in NASCAR history. And they'll likely remain that way forever now that NASCAR has once again reinstated the speed-robbing restrictor plate rule at the fastest tracks on the circuit. Built around a fully tubular (rectangular and round tubing) frame, Davey's 1987 'Birds first took shape on the surface plate at

Davey Allison was a talented young driver destined to accomplish great things on the NASCAR circuit. Though a Winston Cup driver for only a handful of seasons, he managed to rack up an impressive 19 wins. His life was tragically cut short in a freak flying accident well before he reached his prime.

Banjo Matthews' race fabrication shop in Asheville, North Carolina. Rear-steer cars all, Allison's Havoline Fords featured evolutions of the Galaxie front suspension components first perfected by Ralph Moody in 1965. A 9-inch Ford differential was mounted aft and kept in check with a pair of Chevy-truck-style trailing arms and a cross-chassis panhard rod. Massive ventilated disc brakes and multi-piston calipers were mounted all around. The 15x9.5-inch steel rims and massive Goodyear gumballs made the chassis a roller.

Power for Davey's rookie year campaign was cooked up by mechanical alchemist Robert Yates from an evolution of the 351 Cleveland polyangle-valve small-block engine. Alloy heads, a super-secret porting job and equally classified intake manifold, and a single Holley carburetor provided for the ingestion of combustibles. A beefy four-bolt block fitted with a forged alloy and steel reciprocating assembly put those hydrocarbons to work with the help of an external dry-sump sys-

Robert Yates (center) has developed a reputation as a mechanical genius. When still just a "grunt" at Holman & Moody, he built the engine that won the Daytona 500 for LeeRoy Yarbrough in 1969. He also built the engines that powered Davey Allison to fame.

In retrospect, it's clear that the 1987–1988 Thunderbirds that Davey Allison and others campaigned were some of the best all-around stock cars ever built. Many Ford racers on the tour today would give a number of tender body parts to be able to race that body style again. Though gone, those cars are not forgotten. Just take a look at a new Monte Carlo's silhouette and you'll see what we mean.

tem. Stainless steel headers sent the by-products of internal combustion out toward the grandstands without the encumbrance of a muffler. Some 600 to 650 ponies were produced in the process, and that was enough to propel Davey and the car around Daytona and Talladega at speeds in excess of 210 miles per hour.

Tragically, Davey's life was cut short in a freak flying accident just six years after his sparkling rookie season. One of the Thunderbirds he drove in 1987 currently belongs to Kim Haynes of Gastonia, North Carolina.

TECHNICAL INFORMATION

Wheelbase	110 inches
Weight	3,700 pounds
Front Suspension	Screw jack-adjustable, HD coils, fully fabricated control arms, single gas shock per wheel, sway bar
Rear Suspension	Screw jack-adjustable, HD coils, panhard rod, trailing arms, Ford 9-inch differential with floating hubs, single gas shock per wheel
Brakes	Ventilated discs
Engine	358-cubic-inch 1-4V, 650–675-horsepower (unrestricted) V-8
Transmission	Borg Warner Super T-10, floor-shifted, four-speed manual
Speed at Darlington	158 miles per hour

Anthony Joseph Foyt has been called the best all-around racing driver of all time. And perhaps that is true. Foyt's multiple open-wheel victories are legend, as are the four wins he scored in the Indianapolis 500. Foyt has experienced a fair amount of success in the sports car ranks as well, and the record book for the famed 24-hour race in LeMans, France, bears Foyt's name as a winner.

A.J. also spent time on the NASCAR circuit over the years. And not without success. Foyt's earliest ventures into Grand National stock car racing came in the early 1960s. During that era Foyt drove both Dodges and Fords for a number of teams. Win number one of his NASCAR career came in the 1964 Firecracker 400 when he drove a Ray Nichels-prepared Dodge across the stripe first. Fans will recall that 1964 was the year that NASCAR officials decided the non-production 426

Hemi was legal for racing and 426-powered Dodges and Plymouths like the one A.J. drove that year were the class of the field.

Over the years, Foyt has always tried to field the fastest possible race car, and that sometimes resulted in precipitous changes in A.J.'s brand loyalty. That's just what happened in 1965, when Foyt jumped ship to campaign a Ford. It was in 1965 that the always-in-flux NASCAR rules book finally recognized the non-production nature of the 426 Hemi. As a result, that engine was outlawed by the sanctioning body. Chrysler teams were none too thrilled with their reversal of fortune and opted to sit on the sidelines instead of race. With Dodge out of the running, A.J. felt no compunction about hopping into a Banjo Matthews Ford. It was in that number 41 Galaxie that A.J. notched his second straight win in the Firecracker 400 at Daytona.

Anthony Joseph Foyt has driven many makes and models of racing machinery during his lengthy career. In the NASCAR ranks, Foyt has driven Dodges, Fords, Mercurys, Chevrolets, and Oldsmobiles for a number of teams. He drove number 14 Olds Cutlasses like this one during the 1988 season for his own racing organization.

Without doubt, A.J. Foyt is one of the best all-around racing drivers to ever walk down a racing grid. During his NASCAR driving days he won the Firecracker 400 twice, the Daytona 500, the Atlanta 500, and many other events.

It took A.J. five more years to win another Grand National race. The reason for that delay was primarily the part-time, limited-schedule nature of his NASCAR involvement. USAC-style roadster racing was always A.J.'s first love, and he placed those races first on his things-to-do list. As we were saying, A.J.'s next Grand National win came in 1970 at Riverside. Ohioan Jack Bowsher was providing A.J. with NASCAR racing iron in those days, and it was one of Bowsher's blue-and-white number 3 Torinos that A.J. used to best the field of 44 starters at an average speed of 97.450 miles per hour around the always-demanding road course.

In 1971, A.J. signed on with the Wood Brothers team out of Stuart, Virginia. The team was fielding stock-nosed (as opposed to Spoiler II-beaked) 1969 Mercury Cyclones that season. Boss 429 engines powered their red-and-white number 21 fastbacks and made those cars some of the fastest on the circuit. A.J. qualified his Merc on the pole of the 1971 500, for example, with a top speed of 182.744 miles per hour. During the race, Foyt led the pack on six occasions for a total of 36 laps and seemed to be on his way to victory when his car sputtered to a near-stop on the back stretch. He had run out of gas! By the time the sleek Merc coasted into the pits for a refill of Unocal racing gas, Foyt was laps down to the leaders. During the final stages of the race, A.J. was able to unlap himself, but

he was only able to climb back to third before time ran out and the checkered flag fell.

It was an entirely different story just two weeks later at the Miller High Life 500 at Ontario, California. Long-time fans might recall that the track at Ontario (now bull-dozed) was built as an exact replica of the 2.5-mile Indianapolis Motor Speedway oval—right down to the same degree of banking in the turns. A.J. put his intimate knowledge of Indy to good use by qualifying his number 21 Mercury on the pole with a run of 151.711 miles per hour. During the race it was all A.J. He led the race on 10 different occasions, including the most-important final one. A.J. picked up $51,850 for his efforts that day.

Foyt's next win for the Woods came at the Atlanta Motor Speedway in April, when once again he used the impressive number of ponies cranked out by the Tunnel Port 427-powered Mercury to claim the pole position. A.J.'s hot lap of 151.152 miles per hour earned that number one starting slot, and in the race he relied on that power to stay just ahead of Richard Petty for most of the race. When the race was over, it was Foyt's Mercury that was parked in victory lane. When asked about his team's decision to revert to an old Tunnel Port 427 for power, Foyt replied, "The restrictor plates choked the 429 off too much. The Wood boys felt this was the way to go. It turns out they were right." Were they ever.

The front office of a modern NASCAR stocker is a cramped and crowded affair. A form-fitting bucket seat, the all-encompassing roll cage assembly, a fabricated dash full of aftermarket gauges, and the various bits and pieces of control gear all vied for space inside A.J.'s race car and barely left space for Foyt himself.

Foyt's biggest win for the Wood Brothers team was to be one of his last for the team. The race was the 1972 Daytona 500, and A.J. was once again behind the wheel of a Boss 429-powered Mercury Cyclone. In this case, the car was a 1971 iteration of the marque, a version that would prove to be every bit as aerodynamic as the Spoiler IIs and "W" Cyclone the Woods had been racing since 1969.

Though Foyt was not the fastest in qualifying, he came close enough to Bobby Isaac's fast lap of 186.632 miles per hour to sit beside him on the outside pole of the front row. When the race got under way, Foyt wasted little time in assuming the lead. In fact, he took the top spot on the very first lap and basically never looked back. All together, Foyt led a total of seven times for a grand total of 166 laps. Keeping in mind that the whole race consisted of just 200 circuits of the track, you'll understand why newspaper reports of the win called it a lopsided victory. Foyt's win also set an all-time speed record for the 500 of 161.550 miles per hour—a mark that stood until Buddy Baker set a 177.602-mile-per-hour average on his way to winning the 1980 500.

As it turned out, Foyt's biggest enemy in the race was boredom, especially as he led the last 119 laps of the race. After the race, A.J. admitted as much and then said, "I've won at Indy and I've won at LeMans. I've always wanted to win the Daytona 500 because I feel it is the greatest stock car race in the world."

A.J.'s last win for the Woods also turned out to be the last NASCAR victory of his driving career. It came one month after Daytona, back at the Ontario Motor Speedway. Once again at the wheel of the Woods' Boss 429-powered Cyclone, A.J. qualified first for the 1972 Miller High Life 500 and then edged out Bobby Allison's Junior Johnson Chevrolet for the win. Shortly after pocketing the $31,695 purse, A.J. decided to devote more time to his Indy car endeavors and vacated the seat of the number 21 car. David Pearson stepped in to take his place and thus began his legendary stint with the Wood Brothers.

Though A.J. did not score any more NASCAR wins, he continued to make selected appearances on the circuit well into the 1990s. During the late 1980s, he drove Copenhagen-backed number 14 Oldsmobiles, mostly at Daytona and Talladega. One of A.J.'s Cutlasses has been restored and returned to the track in vintage race trim.

TECHNICAL INFORMATION

Wheelbase	110 inches
Weight	3,700 pounds
Front Suspension	Screw jack-adjustable HD coils, fully fabricated control arms, single gas shock per wheel, sway bar
Rear Suspension	Screw jack-adjustable, HD coils, panhard rod, trailing arms, Ford 9-inch differential with floating hubs, single gas shock per wheel
Brakes	Ventilated discs
Engine	358-cubic-inch 1-4V, 600–650-horsepower V-8
Transmission	Borg Warner Super T-10, floor-shifted, four-speed manual
Speed at Darlington	158 miles per hour

Ernie Irvan was basically born on the "wrong" side of the country for stock car racing. Not that there is anything wrong with his Modesto, California, hometown. It's just that Modesto is one heck of a long way from Charlotte and the center of NASCAR country. Even so, Irvan started racing at a very early age. In fact, young Ernie was just 9 when he first took to the track—the go-kart track, that is. That was back in 1968. Seven years later the 16-year-old Irvan moved up to full-sized stock-car-type competition at his local oval. That first real race car was a 1966 Chevelle, and within five races, Ernie had captured his first checkered flag. In 1977, Irvan won the Stockton Speedway track championship by finishing out in front in 15 of the 23 events he entered.

Irvan made the cross-continental jump to North Carolina in 1984 to continue his racing. He won nine events at Concord Speedway that year, along with the National Championship for six-cylinder cars. In 1986 he won eight more races at Concord, and he scored a total of 10 more in late-model Camaros at the Concord and at Tri-County speedways.

He paid for his racing by doing odd jobs around the Charlotte area. For a while he welded seats at the Charlotte Motor Speedway, and he unloaded trucks for Ken Schrader. Irvan's first bite at the Winston Cup apple came in 1987 when he drove Chevrolets for D.K. Ulrich and Mark Reno at five Cup races. Race number one in the big league was at Martinsville in the Goody's 500. Though his 15th-place finish (after starting 24th) didn't immediately catapult him to fame, it was a beginning. Irvan's best finish that first season came at Charlotte in the old National 500, where he drove a Marc Reno Chevrolet to eighth place.

Irvan ran for Rookie-of-the-Year honors in 1988 with the help of Ulrich's U. S. racing team. He made 25

Ernie's Kodak Film Lumina was a sleek combination of fabricated and factory stock body panels that had been draped over a purpose-built racing chassis. Like all Cup cars of its day, it was more of a silhouette car than a "stock" racing vehicle.

Ernie Irvan was born far from the Carolinas and the bull rings from which the National Association of Stock Car Automobile Racing sprang. Yet he still developed into one of the best fender rubbers on the Winston Cup circuit. Proof of that fact is the victory he scored with this Lumina in the 1991 Daytona 500.

Huge ventilated discs and multi-piston calipers were mounted beneath Irvan's yellow Chevrolet and helped scrub speed for pit lane entry. Once the car was at speed on the track, those impressive stoppers didn't get much use since Ernie was usually charging for the front with his right foot flat on the floor.

starts that year and won $96,370 in prize money, but he missed out on the Rookie title by a mere three points.

Ernie started 29 Winston Cup events in 1989, and along the way, he also raced at selected events on the ARCA and Busch circuits. He posted his first stock car superspeedway win in an ARCA race at Atlanta that year.

Ernie got his first big-time ride in 1990, when he was signed to drive the Morgan-McClure Kodak Films Olds in March. His first outing for the team at Atlanta was simply sensational. Rain canceled qualifying for the race that year so the field was set up according to points standings, and that meant that Irvan was relegated to starting 30th. Even so, by lap 232, Irvan had the bright yellow number 4 car in the lead. He dueled with Morgan Shepherd's Bud Moore Ford and Dale Earnhardt's Chevrolet for the rest of the race and ultimately finished third. After the race, team owner Larry McClure said, "The way he (Irvan) handled the car didn't surprise me at all. This should lay to rest all speculation about why I hired him."

Irvan turned in a string of credible finishes in the ensuing races, including fourths at Talladega and Charlotte and a second at Charlotte, before scoring the first

Though street-going 1991 Luminas came equipped with sleepy front-wheel-drive V-6 drivetrains, racing versions like the car Irvan parked in victory lane at the Daytona 500 featured a fire-breathing small-block Chevrolet engine and a conventional rear-drive chassis.

win of his Winston Cup career. That triumph came at Bristol in the Busch 500. The Kodak team had shifted to Chevrolet sheet metal several races before the race in Bristol, and Irvan used the new car's improved aerodynamics to qualify in the sixth slot. When the flag fell, Irvan began to methodically work toward the front, a position he reached on lap 68. He took the lead for the final time on lap 411, when current leader Earnhardt was forced to pit with a cut tire. Ernie never looked back. He crossed the stripe just ahead of runner-up Rusty Wallace.

Ernie backed up that first win with a second-place finish just one week later in the Southern 500. He finished the season ninth in points, with one win and five other top-five finishes. Better things were waiting for Irvan just around the corner.

The 1991 season found Irvan once again at the helm of the Morgan-McClure Chevrolet. When the NASCAR circus rolled back into Daytona for the 500, Irvan had one of the strongest cars in the garage area. He made that fact known loud and clear by qualifying just a tick slower than pole-winner Davey Allison's hot lap of 195.955 miles per hour. With a front-row berth assured, Ernie then went on to finish second in his qualifying race.

When the green flag fell on race day, Irvan drove a smart race, conserving his Chevrolet for the closing laps. He took the lead for the first time on lap 125 (of 200). Later in the race, Irvan took the lead for a final time after a shunt bunched the field under the yellow. The green came out on lap 195, and Irvan surprised the crowd by rocketing around Earnhardt for the top spot. Three laps later Earnhardt got out of shape trying to catch Irvan's speeding Chevrolet, and the resulting crash brought out the yellow for the final time, locking Irvan into the first place. Earnhardt's antics left everybody in a funk— except Irvan. After the race Irvan said, "I feel like I've just won the biggest race in the world." And so he had.

TECHNICAL INFORMATION

Wheelbase	110 inches
Weight	3,500 pounds
Front Suspension	Screw jack-adjustable, HD coils and fabricated control arms, single gas shock per wheel, sway bar
Rear Suspension	Screw jack-adjustable, HD coils, panhard rod, trailing arms, Ford 9-inch differential with floating hubs, single gas shock per wheel
Brakes	Ventilated discs
Engine	358-cubic-inch 1-4V, 700-horsepower V-8
Transmission	Borg Warner Super T-10, floor-shifted, four-speed manual
Speed at Darlington	159 miles per hour

As fans will recall, Irvan continued on with the Kodak team until Davey Allison's untimely death opened up a seat at Robert Yates Racing. Ernie has continued his winning ways since slipping behind the wheel of the Havoline Ford. He has also overcome a near-fatal practice crash at Michigan. To date, Irvan has scored a total of 14 wins on the Winston Cup circuit. It's likely that he'll score many more.

Cotton Owens scored Pontiac's first Grand National stock car win in February of 1957 at the fabled beach race in Daytona. By 1961, cars from the "Indian Head" division of General Motors were regular visitors in victory lane and were the fastest stock cars on the circuit. At the dawn of the 1960s, Marvin Panch and Fireball Roberts won back-to-back Daytona 500s, and Ford teams shuddered at the thought of having to match the top speed displayed by superduty Catalinas.

But suddenly, all of that changed in 1963 when General Motors pulled the factory-sponsorship rug from beneath all of the Poncho (and Chevrolet) teams on the circuit. As a result, all Pontiac fans could do was think about what might have been for most of the balance of the decade. In fact, it wasn't until 1981 that a Pontiac once again found the way to a NASCAR victory lane. Since that time, Pontiac drivers like Richard Petty (now

retired), his son Kyle, and Rusty Wallace have carried on the winning Pontiac tradition first established by Owens, Roberts, and Panch.

The year 1996 marked the introduction of an all-new Grand Prix. Based on the same street-going platform as the new Monte Carlo, a contemporary Winston Cup Grand Prix is significantly swoopier and more aerodynamic than the Lumina-based GPs it replaced.

Like its Chevrolet and Fomoco garage mates, a modern Grand Prix is built over a custom racing chassis that has little if anything in common with the one found under a street-going car.

A mix and match of Ford and Chevrolet components are used to assemble the car's suspension. Like just about all cars on the tour today, most Winston Cup Grand Prixes rely on Chevrolet Camaro/Chevelle-evolved front-steer (tie rod ahead of spindle) front suspension components. A Ford 9-inch differential is

Like all modern Cup cars, a contemporary Grand Prix began life as just so much mild steel tubing on the floor of a fabrication shop. Thousands of man-hours later, that pile of metal stock is a 200-mile-per-hour stock car and ready to race.

Swoopy and rounded off on just about every edge, a modern WC Grand Prix is as much a creature of the wind tunnel as it is of the styling studio. The new-for-1996 design featured a "laid-down" front clip, slap sides, and a raised rounded bustle—all features designed to decrease power-robbing aerodynamic drag.

mounted at rear and works in concert with Chevy truck-style trailing arms and a panhard rod. Stubby screw jack-adjustable coil springs and a quartet of gas-charged shocks are mounted at all four corners. Super heavy-duty multi-piston calipers and ventilated discs are similarly situated. Fifteen-inch steel rims and sticky Goodyear radials make the chassis a roller.

Though race programs may list the cars that Bobby Hamilton currently drives for Petty Enterprises as Pontiacs, in truth, those cars rely on Chevrolet small-block engines for motorvation. Like all Chevrolet engines since 1955, the engines used in the number 43 car (and other GPs on the tour) feature inline valves, cast alloy heads, and a beefy four-bolt main-journaled block. A forged everything reciprocating assembly resides within those castings and receives timing inputs from a roller-lifter-equipped camshaft.

When breathing through an unrestricted, single four-barrel carburetor (with 1 11/16-inch throttle bores) and a single-plane intake manifold, a "Pontiac" small block can be relied on for upwards of 700 horsepower. Coupled with a Grand Prix' sleek aero-silhouette, those ponies can propel a race-spec chassis to speeds in excess of 220 miles per hour at Daytona and Talladega. Unfortunately, the desire for maximum advertiser exposure (read: keeping cars bunched up for the camera), which NASCAR expresses as a concern for "safety," has resulted in the rules-mandated use of horsepower-robbing restrictor plates at those tracks, so actual speeds are significantly less. Even so, speeds in excess of 190 miles per hour are still on tap when the

TECHNICAL INFORMATION

Wheelbase	110 inches
Weight	3,400 pounds
Front Suspension	Screw jack-adjustable, HD coils, fully fabricated control arms, single gas shock per wheel, sway bar
Rear Suspension	Screw jack-adjustable, HD coils, panhard rod, trailing arms, Ford 9-inch differential with floating hubs, single gas shock per wheel
Brakes	Ventilated discs
Engine	358-cubic-inch 1-4V, 700-horsepower V-8
Transmission	Borg Warner Super T-10, floor-shifted, four-speed manual
Speed at Darlington	159 miles per hour

Winston Cup circus rolls into Daytona and Talladega.

Though at this writing the new Grand Prix body style has yet to record its first NASCAR win, it's doubtless that trips to victory lane will come.

1996 CHEVROLET MONTE CARLO

Though there have been long stretches of NASCAR competition when Chevrolet-badged competition cars were absent from the NASCAR garage area, the Bow Tie division of General Motors can still claim more stock car victories than any other manufacturer save for Ford. Since Fonty Flock recorded Chevy's very first Grand National win in 1955, Chevrolet drivers have campaigned a wide variety of body styles in NASCAR competition. Impalas, Bel Aires, Luminas, and Chevelles have all, at one time or another, worn NASCAR war paint. Even so, the winningest Chevrolet nameplate has been the Monte Carlo.

Junior Johnson-built number 3 Monte Carlos made that body style's competition debut during the 1971 season, and soon Chevrolets were a regular fixture in victory lane. During the 1970s, the back-door help provided by Chevrolet R&D persuaded many former Ford and Chryco drivers to switch to Bow Tie power, and for nearly a decade, GM cars had just about an exclusive lock on the victory lane gate. Dale Earnhardt, Darrell Waltrip, Bobby Allison, and Terry Labonte beat just about all comers for Chevrolet in the 1980s, for exam-

ple, and won all but one of the national championships contested from 1980 to 1989.

And that's pretty much been the story for the 1990s, as well. With the exception of Alan Kulwicki's 1992 Winston Cup championship for Ford, Dale Earnhardt, Jeff Gordon, and Terry Labonte have had exclusive control of the national driving championship since 1990. And that dominance is likely to continue throughout the rest of the decade.

Gordon's 1995 title and the wins scored that season and since were all made possible by competition cars that once again bear the famed Monte Carlo badge. Based on the new-for-1995 front-wheel-drive Monte Carlo passenger car, the latest Winston Cup iteration of the breed is the swoopiest and most aerodynamic race car ever. Especially so since the sanctioning body allowed Chevy teams significant aero-concessions in advance of their debut at Daytona in 1995. With parity as the stated goal, the NASCAR rules book was altered to permit the new Monte Carlo body style to be significantly widened. That change, coupled with a number of other modifications, has made the new car the aero-

Chevrolet rolled out an all-new Monte Carlo just in time for the 1995 NASCAR season, and, boy, was it a winner right out of the box. Blessed with good lines by the GM styling studio and even better race track aerodynamics, thanks to significant concessions granted by the sanctioning body (in the name of "parity"), the new Chevrolet was an immediate success.

One of the big changes away from "stock" permitted by the 1995–1996 NASCAR rules book, and which worked out well for Monte Carlo teams, was their ability to significantly widen the rear sheet metal shape of the new body style. The extra 6 inches NASCAR gave Chevy teams in rear-end width gave the cars an aerodynamic advantage that left Ford and Pontiac drivers in the dust.

It will come as no surprise that drivers like Dale Earnhardt and Darrell Waltrip relied on high-horsepower iterations of the Chevrolet small-block engine for power during the 1995 and 1996 seasons. In contemporary 17:1-compression-ratio trim, a "mouse" motor cranks out a monstrous 750-plus horsepower.

sheet metal stock. Thousands of hours of welding, English wheel work, and sheet metal fabrication go into the construction of every Winston Cup Monte Carlo, and no small amount of attention is spent on the car's final aerodynamic silhouette. Though a race-spec Monte Carlo may appear (from the grandstands, at least) to be strikingly stock, in reality, most of such a car's sheet metal was formed by hand out of flat stock. Truth be known, only the hood panel, roof panel, and trunk lid are "stock"—the rest of the car being wholly a creation of the metal crafter.

The completed chassis of a Winston Cup Monte Carlo usually rolls on a mixture of Chevrolet- and Ford-evolved suspension components. Modern front-steer cars (and most cars in a Winston Cup garage are front-steer these days) roll on fabricated control arms that essentially recreate the geometry found under a 1970s Chevelle. Kidney pummeling screw jack-adjustable coil springs, a pair of gas-charged shocks, and a thick, spline-ended sway bar make up the balance of the car's front suspension. A full-floater Ford 9-inch differential is mounted aft, and it is centered under the chassis with a pair of trailing arms evolved from the Chevrolet truck line and another pair of

dynamic equal of Ford's Thunderbird and saved the sanctioning body from the unhappy prospect of a competition field comprised solely of Ford products.

Like all Cup cars, the new Monte Carlos on the tour began as an assortment of mild steel tubes and screw jack-adjustable coils. A panhard rod and two more gas shocks make up the balance of a Winston Cup Monte Carlo's rear suspension.

A high-powered evolution of the familiar Chevrolet small-block engine is used for power. Like all such engines since 1955, a Winston Cup "mouse" motor features inline valves, pedestal-mounted rocker arms, and a camshaft mounted in the center of the block. Alloy is used for the head castings, while conventional cast iron is mandated for the block. Four-bolt main caps provide the resolve for extended periods of high-rpm operation, and a dry-sump oiling system makes that rotation possible.

The fires of internal combustion are fed by a single Holley carburetor and a single-plane, high-rise-style intake manifold. A pointless, high-voltage ignition system (with redundancy features) is used to spark those fires, and the spent gases thus produced are carried toward the grandstands through a set of stainless steel tubular headers.

In race trim, a modern Monte Carlo "stock" car is capable of speeds in excess of 190 miles per hour even when choked with one of NASCAR's infernal restrictor plates. Blessed by the NASCAR rules book and graced with both beauty and speed, the modern Monte Carlos fielded by Dale Earnhardt and others on the Winston Cup circuit will no doubt continue to carry the Chevrolet Bow Tie into victory lane for years to come.

TECHNICAL INFORMATION

Wheelbase	110 inches
Weight	3,400 pounds
Front Suspension	Screw jack-adjustable, HD coils and fabricated control arms, single gas shock per wheel, sway bar
Rear Suspension	Screw jack-adjustable, HD coils, panhard rod, trailing arms, Ford 9-inch differential with floating hubs, single gas shock per wheel
Brakes	Ventilated discs
Engine	358-cubic-inch 1-4V, 700-horsepower V-8
Transmission	Borg Warner Super T-10, floor-shifted, four-speed manual
Speed at Darlington	159 miles per hour

The new Monte Carlo body style is characterized by a low-profile front fascia that sweeps up from the pavement in a relatively unbroken arc. A laid-back windscreen then directs the onrushing air up and over the rounded roof panel to the raised and widened rear deck. The car is every bit as aerodynamic as Ford's 1987–1988 Thunderbirds and carries more than a passing resemblance to those cars.

1996 FORD THUNDERBIRD

The Ford Motor Company has been a presence in NASCAR circles since the very first strictly stock race way back in 1949. And since the dust settled after the conclusion of that dirt track event, Ford drivers have visited victory lane more times than anyone else.

Today Ford *pilotos* like Dale Jarrett, Ernie Irvan, Mark Martin, Bill Elliott, and Rusty Wallace roll into battle in sleek new Thunderbirds. Truth be known, those 3,400-pound Winston Cup "stockers" are far from stock. In fact, with the exception of hood, trunk, and roof panels, there's precious little of a modern stock car that ever came out of a UAW plant.

Instead, a modern 110-inch-wheelbase Thunderbird starts its competitive life as little more than an assortment of rectangular tubing on the surface plate of a fabrication facility. Once that purpose-built chassis has taken shape,

The contemporary Ford Thunderbird represents more than 30 years of mechanical evolution. Like the 1965 Galaxies that preceded it on the tour, a modern WC 'Bird rolls on unequal-length "A" frames at the bow, a full-floater live axle at the stern, and screw jack-adjusted coil springs all around. That having been said, a modern Ford is aerodynamically light years ahead of its boxy Galaxie progenitors.

Thunderbirds like the ones campaigned by Bud Moore and Robert Yates in the 1996 season were powered by a high-horsepower version of the 351 Cleveland engine. In NASCAR trim, that engine displaced 358 cubic inches, came topped with alloy heads and a single Holley carburetor, and featured a beefy four-bolt main-journaled bottom end. Tuning wizards like Yates and Jack Roush were able to coax nearly 800 horsepower out of their "small blocks" in 1996.

it is fitted with suspension components. Though Ralph Moody's 1965 Galaxie-perfected rear-steer componentry used to be the industry standard, most modern (circa 1996) Ford stockers roll on front-steer suspension members that evolved from the Chevrolet Chevelle. Screw jack-adjusted coils and a splined, through-chassis sway bar round out the front suspension.

A Ford 9-inch differential is the primary feature of a modern T-Bird's rear suspension. It is located under the rear frame rails by a set of Chevy truck-derived trailing arms, a pair of screw jack-adjustable coil springs, and a cross-chassis panhard rod.

Huge multi-piston calipers are mounted at all four corners. They act on equally massive, ventilated discs and are capable of scrubbing off speed at an impressive rate. Wheels are a NASCAR-standard 15x9.5-inch stamped steel rims carrying sticky Goodyear racing slicks that make the entire package a roller.

A tremendous amount of time is spent on the sheet-metal skin that is used to cloak a modern Winston Cup Thunderbird's chassis. Hours of wind-tunnel time coupled with the requirements of an ever-changing NASCAR rules book determine a T-Bird's ultimate configuration. The reason for all the ink and effort expended on a car's cosmetic silhouette is, of course, aerodynamics. In a competition world where a car's ultimate horsepower is determined by the sanctioning body, minor sheet-metal modifications can make the difference between winning and losing.

Power for the whole package comes from a racing evolution of the 351 Cleveland small-block engine that Bud Moore first perfected in the early 1970s. These high-rpm powerplants are built around a decidedly non-production four-bolt block that mounts a knife-edged, forged steel crank and an octet of forged rods. Domed pistons compress incoming combustibles at a rules mandated 14:1 ratio under the governance of a roller cam.

Heavily massaged alloy head castings first cooked up by Robert Yates are used to cap off the short block, and these polyangle-valved flow controllers received thousands of hours of attention during engine assembly. A single four-barrel carburetor and a high-rise-style intake manifold round out the intake tract. Other underhood appointments in a Winston Cup 'Bird's engine bay include a multi-stage dry-sump system, a high-energy ignition system with back-ups, and a set of

Though not as aerodynamically efficient as the 1987–1988 Thunderbird body style, a 1996 Ford Cup car was still no slouch in the air management department. Deceptively stock-looking at first blush, a modern Thunderbird's slippery silhouette contained very few regular-production-based body panels.

tubular headers. Depending on the track, a race-spec Cleveland engine is backed up either with a race-ready BW T-10 four-speed or an evolution of Ford's trusty Top Loader transmission.

With restrictor plate in place, a modern Winston Cup Ford engine is choked down to just 550 horsepower or so. In unrestricted form, more than 750 ponies are available for track work.

Though far from stock, and subject to increasingly more-stringent sanctioning-body regulation, the modern Winston Cup Thunderbirds on the circuit are the direct descendants of the Holman & Moody Galaxies, Cyclones, and Talladegas that dominated the Grand National scene during the 1960s and 1970s. And like those mechanical predecessors, the Thunderbirds driven by Messrs. Irvan, Elliott, and Jarrett are trend-setting winners that will show the way to stock car racing's future.

Modern NASCAR rules books spend more than a little time and ink on the proper configuration and mounting position for a car's rear-deck spoiler. A 45-degree angle of attack has most recently been required for those large, downforce-producing alloy panels.

TECHNICAL INFORMATION

Wheelbase	110 inches
Weight	3,400 pounds
Front Suspension	Screw jack-adjustable, HD coils, fully fabricated control arms, sway bar, single gas shock per wheel
Rear Suspension	Screw jack-adjustable, HD coils, trailing arms, panhard rod, Ford 9-inch differential with floating hubs, single gas shock per wheel
Brakes	Ventilated discs
Engine	358-cubic-inch 1-4V, 700-horsepower (unrestricted) V-8
Transmission	Borg Warner Super T-10, floor-shifted, four-speed manual
Speed at Darlington	159 miles per hour

While automotive competition will always encompass a certain number of unavoidable risks, the rules-mandated roll cage found in a contemporary Winston Cup Ford (or Chevy or Pontiac) makes the close-quarters action—typical of stock car racing—a lot less worrisome. When accidents do happen, drivers like Bill Elliott and Ernie Irvan more often than not walk away.

INDEX